MEETING TOM BRADY

MEETING TOM

One Man's Quest for
Truth, Enlightenment,
and a Simple Game of
Catch with the Patriots
Quarterback

RICHARD J. KING

with illustrations by the author

BRADY

ForeEdge

ForeEdge

An imprint of University Press of New England

www.upne.com

© 2015 Richard J. King

All rights reserved

Manufactured in the United States of America

Designed by Richard Hendel

Typeset in Utopia, Franklin Gothic, Champion, and Clan

by Passumpsic Publishing

For permission to reproduce any of the material in this book,
contact Permissions, University Press of New England, One Court Street,
Suite 250, Lebanon NH 03766; or visit www.upne.com

This book is a memoir. It contains the author's recollections.
Certain names and identifying characteristics have been changed
and certain incidents have been compressed or reordered.

Library of Congress Cataloging-in-Publication Data
available upon request.

5 4 3 2 1

TO UNCLE FRANK

And to all the people associated with

Westerly Area Rest Meals. A quarter of the

author's proceeds for the book will be donated

to this organization.

The mass of men lead lives of quiet desperation.

—HENRY DAVID THOREAU,

   fan of the patriots of New England

CONTENTS

PREFACE

On the night of February 1, 2015, the New England Patriots trailed in the fourth quarter by ten points, a deficit from which no Super Bowl champion had ever recovered. Their quarterback, Tom Brady, faced third and fourteen. He scanned across the line at the young and brash Seattle Seahawks, the reigning champions and the stingiest defense in the NFL. Brady hollered signals over the bellows of more than seventy thousand fans at the University of Phoenix Stadium in Glendale, Arizona. More than 121 million other people watched him on television or on a tablet or on some other device, which is, as far as I can figure, the largest audience for a single live performance of any kind in human history.

From his own twenty-eight-yard line, Tom Brady took the snap, stepped back, then had to run forward in the pocket as the Seattle linemen grappled in. He planted and slung a dart down the field to Julian Edelman, his most trusted receiver, who snagged the football for a long first down and held on to it, somehow, even as Seattle's bruising safety Kam Chancellor cracked into him at full speed. Still alive. From here, Brady led his team down the field for a touchdown. When the Seahawks gave the ball right back, Brady drove his offense a second time, methodically and artfully, without missing a single completion — a perfect eight for eight — putting his team ahead 28–24 with a fourth touchdown pass, this last one to Edelman.

Brady jogged to the sideline, took off his helmet, and sat on the bench. With less than a minute to play, he watched a Seattle receiver with the appropriate surname of Kearse make an absurd, falling, bobbling, deep sideline catch after the football bounced off his knee, putting Seattle within a few yards of the goal line. (I crawled behind the bar to try to hide from my own despair, because this threatened to be the *third* time in a row that an impossible catch had whisked away a Patriots victory when Brady had them ahead in the closing minutes of a Super Bowl.) If Brady and the Patriots lost yet another championship, all the questions — about his age, his abilities, his toughness, and his integrity — that had dogged him for the last several seasons would not only spread, they would solidify.

Then the gods of fortune struck once more. With twenty-eight seconds left, a rookie third-string cornerback named Malcolm Butler preserved the win with a sensational and shocking interception on the Patriots' own goal line. (I saw this only on replay, because I had rested my forehead on a steel sink.)

Tom Brady walked off that field, under the rain of ticker tape, earning a fourth Super Bowl ring, a third Super Bowl MVP, and a string of postseason records, including the most playoff fourth-quarter comebacks in the history of the sport. He is now, if not *the* greatest, undeniably on the shortest of lists of the best to ever play the game. The *Sports Illustrated* cover that week featured him peering wide-eyed over the swarming Seattle defense as he released the football from his fingertips toward the viewer, toward you, toward me, toward the one who would catch his pass for another first down. The headline read: "On to Immortality."

But as the offseason of celebration wore on, an FBI-style enquiry reported that Tom Brady probably knew that two locker-room equipment managers had softened the footballs to his preference, outside the rules, before the AFC championship game. Maybe they had done the same in prior games. The controversy, which became known as "Deflategate," slashed the first deep cut in the quarterback's flawless image and historic career. Smelling blood in the water, a frenzy of media, fans, and current and former players surged in to take a bite. The league gave Brady and the New England Patriots one of the stiffest punishments it had ever handed down. For my part, I'm still trying to parse out exactly what happened —both with the slightly under-inflated footballs and with the ferocity and ubiquity of public response. To be honest, I was more disappointed in him when he did not travel with his team to the White House in the spring—when President Obama honored the Patriots for their Super Bowl victory.

None of this matters, of course, against the scale of real concerns in the world, such as hunger and terrorism and police brutality and the downhill speed of environmental degradation. But Brady's success in this Super Bowl—or maybe more importantly, his evasion of another defeat—meant a hell of a lot to me. And it still does, however scarred. Because when I got it into my head that I needed to meet Tom Brady two years earlier, in the spring of 2013, I didn't know all this was going to happen. In fact, several analysts doubted if Brady had much good football left in him at all. He was in his mid-thirties—younger than I was, but a dinosaur in the NFL. He was the oldest player on his team by several years. Some analysts declared that Tom Brady had enjoyed a Hall of Fame career, but it was time to hang up the cleats. Two years ago, they said Tom Brady was in decline. I knew I was.

1

STAYING OFF
THE CRAZY
LIST

JULY 26, 2013 / 5:30 A.M.
FOXBOROUGH, MASSACHUSETTS

I'm parked here beside Gillette Stadium, where the New England Patriots play football. It's raining, but sitting here in my van I have a perfect seat to watch the *Mike and Mike* early morning radio show, which is on location to cover the opening of training camp. Here's a bird's-eye view:

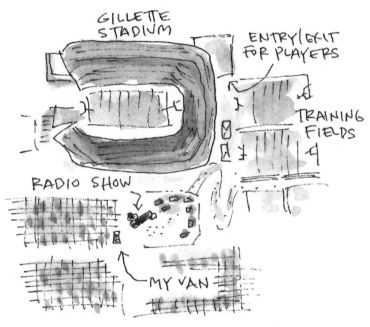

I am stating here, for the record, that I was the first fan to show up this season. A few others arrived this morning before I pulled up at 5:00, but I was here last night. Ruby and I parked in the lot, closed the curtains, and set up the bed inside. I parked right next to a porta-potty, and I was dozing off when I got the knock on the glass. A flashlight in the window. Ruby didn't bark. The security guy said we couldn't stay.

So I drove away from the stadium and found a campground, where I asked the night watchman if I could park.

I look even sketchier these days in the van because the power window on the driver's door is stuck shut, so I have to talk through the small swing window over the side-view mirror. The night watchman let me park in an outer lot and wouldn't take any money. So in the end I got to the stadium this dark early morning after a few other people. But again, I was here last night to sleep out.

Here's my van, a 1988 Volkswagen Vanagon camper with a pop-top (that has a few holes in the canvas), a stove (that doesn't work), and a fridge (that cools cautiously):

The sun hasn't come up yet, but dozens of people are already outside to watch the radio show. The gates to the field open in a few hours. As the show begins, workers and concessionaires prepare for the crowds to arrive by setting up their tables under individual tents. Two women set up a stand where they're going to sell coffee—for which I am desperate—while stadium staff assemble a variety of free entertainments, such as a blow-up bouncy castle for kids.

One of the radio announcers, one of the Mikes, looks out at the Patriots fans, who in the half-light wear useless plastic ponchos while standing next to chairs that are too wet for sitting down. "You people are crazy!" he says. This brings muted cheers. It's clear he's only half kidding.

At each commercial break, a producer walks onto the stage. She tries to rile the little crowd with easy trivia questions, gifts, and exhortations to cheer loudly when the announcers return live. While Mike and Mike muse about how the New England Patriots star quarterback might possibly put together any offense this year with all his receivers gone, the producer walks off under an umbrella with a dour face and a cigarette. Mike and Mike each predict that the Patriots will win ten games and lose six this year.

My friend Lenny, the commissioner of our Middle-aged Football League, the MFL, likes to say that malls and football games are the only remaining true melting pots of America. There's some truth to that this morning. I'm not proud to admit this, but I expected only pasty-white overweight men. As the rain eases and the players in their locker room get ready to jog out onto the practice field, I watch from my van as all types of fans file in: fit sporty people, families with little kids, Asian families, Indian families, African American families, and WASPy families. Even a clique of young female fashionistas arrives, arm in arm, wearing beaded Patriots boots and sparkly outfits as if bopping over to a dance club. I see kids holding footballs like teddy bears. There go a dad, mom, and their son all wearing Tom Brady number-twelve jerseys. Another boy has an "I love Tom Brady" sign. One young woman carries a poster board that says, "Call me Gisele" — which she surely is doubling as a *Moby-Dick* reference.

9:50 P.M. / MYSTIC, CONNECTICUT

I'm back at the house now, on the living room couch with Ruby. Everyone else is asleep. The van made it to Foxborough and back, but the speedometer stopped working as I went through Providence.

This morning, after I had my fill of the radio show, I took Ruby for a walk to let her mark Gillette Stadium as her new territory. After she curled up into her fleece blanket in the back seat for a morning nap, I walked down to the practice field. Here I was greeted with a picture of pure pigskin promise! In the summer rain the players' sharp blue and white uniforms and the fans' yellow and green rain jackets popped against the gray sky. In the stands or on the grass hill behind the end zone, each fan found a quality seat with a close view of the players. I watched Coach Bill Belichick evaluating his new charges as he spun his whistle around his fingers, clockwise then counterclockwise, then back again. Star nose tackle Vince Wilfork, weighing some 330 pounds, lumbered across the field.

A tent behind the stands sold Patriots gear at super-cheap prices. I bought a cap for five bucks. It would be hard to overstate my pleasure in this acquisition. I don't think I've worn a piece of gear with a professional team's logo since I was in middle school. It fits perfectly, I'm wearing it right now, and I just might sleep with it. What I love especially is that it has no words, simply the old "Pat Patriot" logo.

Stadium staff gave out paper rosters with the names of the ninety players and their numbers. A few serious fans, usually older men by themselves, studied this sheet over their glasses and then squinted up to find the uniforms on the field. Is this me in twenty years? By the start of the season only fifty-three of these players will make the team.

When he jogged in, I was settling myself on a bench. I was reveling in my new hat and trying to identify the new receivers. I heard a cheer from the crowd and looked over. Tom Brady entered like a goddamn matador. Quarterbacks in training camps across the league wear scarlet red jerseys so everyone knows not to hit these guys in practice. The backup quarterbacks hadn't come out yet, so Brady was the only splash of red on the whole green field. One hand carried his helmet, while the other he raised open-palmed to acknowledge The People. I watched him with binoculars. He smiled with his head tilted in slight deference to the applause. He was very tan. He and his supermodel wife Gisele Bündchen have a vacation house in Costa Rica. It would not have felt incongruous if those fans assembled on the grass had thrown bouquets to Tom Brady. Or even if his fellow players had tossed a few rose petals.

Brady pumped his fist, the crowd cheered louder, and then he stepped in among his teammates. The crowd settled down. Practice continued. The players jogged through a few kickoff formations, a few loose plays on offense and defense, and then general drills by position.

While we common fans sat in the rain on the aluminum stands or on the wet grass of the hill, a different class of spectator sat dry under two tents farther down on the same hill, overlooking the field. One tent seemed to shelter VIPs. The other kept the press corps dry. In the press tent, men and women sat three rows deep as they watched and scribbled in notebooks and clicked on electronic devices. Their focus was threefold: (1) record or reflect on anything done or not done by Tom Brady; (2) record or reflect on anything done or not done by the compelling new backup to Tom Brady; and (3) record or reflect on anything done or not done by the individuals in the gaggle of unknown receivers, which included one second-string Patriot wideout remaining from last year's team, several rookies and castaway veterans from other teams, and one expensive new-hire from the St. Louis Rams. All these hopefuls will compete during the next several weeks to make up Tom Brady's new offensive quiver. Every single pass and catch or (gasp!) drop revealed something Twitter-worthy about the evolving chemistry—or lack thereof—with Tom Brady and these tryout receivers.

How do I get a seat under one of those tents?

At one point during practice, Patriots owner Robert Kraft strode onto the field with his son, Patriots president Jonathan

Kraft. The two men wore jeans and Oxford shirts in the way politicians dress down when they seek to appeal to a certain audience. They walked under umbrellas with a couple of other VIPs. One of their party was an exceptionally attractive young woman wearing a black miniskirt and high spiked heels. Wobbling a bit on the grass, she watched and chatted.

Brady trotted over with his helmet off to greet the owners. Perhaps they had truly not seen each other in the team buildings in recent days, but this hello on the field seemed a bit of theater for the *Boston Globe* reporters and the other press under the tent. Headline: "Patriots Star Shakes Hands with Owners to Signal New Campaign for Trophy." Through my binoculars I saw Brady shake the young woman's hand. She flushed, smiled hugely, and kept smiling. I kept looking back at her. For easily fifteen minutes more she smiled.

Mr. Brady, I'm quite certain I've never have had that sort of effect on a woman. Does that feeling, when you see a woman react to you like that — I presume it's some mixture of pride and virility — does it wear off after so many repetitions of smiles and blushes and gestures and hand-painted signs and women wearing as revealingly as possible a Patriots jersey with your number and your name on the back? Would you tell me just one little juicy story? Off the record, of course.

Several busloads of counselors and kids from day camps came to this first day of training camp, too. The children ran around behind the stands and stood at the lower rail beside the field. Apparently after each practice a few players stick around for a while to sign autographs. I wasn't sure exactly when the signing was going to happen, or even if Brady would be one of the players to sign autographs on the first day.

I felt a little conflicted anyway about the prospect of standing in a collection of kids trying to get Brady's autograph, even though, ironically, I've begun this mission to meet the man. I grew up outside of Philadelphia, so when I was about ten years old, my dad took me to an Eagles game. A player was signing footballs and whatever else kids brought. I wanted my dad to help me shove in there, to do it for me, but he wouldn't. I was disappointed in him for not muscling me to the front. But I realize now that it wasn't that he didn't want to be forthright; he just felt odd grubbing for a signature from another man, a *younger* man. I mean, my dad was a huge athlete growing up, and he still loves sports. I see his perspective now. I'm sure that's how it was. After all these years, I can see his facial expression and can read it now, even though I've never talked to him about that moment. I see also something in my dad's face that said: "Son, why don't you ever look at me like that?"

I assume I'll feel the same when my daughter is old enough to start choosing her heroes.

After I had been down beside the field for an hour or so this morning, I got hungry and wanted to make sure Ruby was okay, in case they were going to tow the van because it was too close to the radio show when they disassembled. I bought a grilled sausage and hustled up to walk my dog again. If the training camp staff had posted a schedule about when exactly practice was ending and signatures were to begin, I couldn't find it.

So by the time I was walking back down to the field, everything had finished. I wove against a tide of outbound fans. I overheard that Brady had been one of the people signing autographs. Argh. A wasted opportunity. I could've stood at least a few yards from him. Observed how he interacted. I could've listened to him talk off-camera. Maybe I could've handed him a letter introducing myself? Ridiculous. What would he do with that? Stick it in his sock? Would he even accept a paper letter from an unknown fan?

I had about another hour before I needed to start driving home, so I hurried over to the Patriots Shop. I bought a magnet in the shape of a Patriots helmet for the back of the van. Then I booked it up to the Patriots Hall of Fame. Most impressive here was the exhibition of *Sports Illustrated* covers on which Brady has appeared. Seventeen times over eleven years. His first and second were after his first Super Bowl win in 2002. In the April issue he sits without a shirt, holding a football with the headline: "The Natural." On another cover in 2005 he is the magazine's "Sportsman of the Year." His most recent was in January 2012, before his fifth Super Bowl appearance, with the headline: "Rematch!"

And then I saw what I call "The Photograph." At the Patriots Hall of Fame they have a little corner to evoke what it's like after a Super Bowl win: ticker tape on the floor, ticker tape falling from the ceiling, three replicas of their three Super Bowl trophies under glass, and big images on big screens with highlight videos and still photographs. In the cycle of images, they cut to that one photograph of Tom Brady that has stuck with me for so many years and in many ways has been a catalyst for this endeavor.

The image is of him at only twenty-four years old, at the time the youngest quarterback ever to win the Super Bowl. Only a few minutes earlier, he had also been crowned the Most Valuable Player of the game. He's looking around at seventy-five thousand people shouting their heads off, and he must be at least obliquely aware that some eighty-five *million* more watch him on television. He sees fireworks, the dazzle glitter of camera flashes, and squalls of red, white, and blue ticker tape. Inside the New Orleans Superdome on this night in 2002, as the United States remains stunned from the events of 9–11, all-American boy Tom Brady has skyrocketed from backup to hero in a matter of months, culminating in this precise moment. He's wearing a Super Bowl champion T-shirt and a Super Bowl champion hat on backwards. Stripes of eye-black remain on his face. With both hands he cups the back of his head in awe.

Certainly I've had moments of which I've been proud at work or with my writing and illustrations, or with some other relatively minor accomplishment, but that photograph of young Brady captures an instant of pure elation and glory. The Photograph and its essential, almost existential appeal to me is not, I hope, so much about fame. Because in The Photograph, Tom Brady's smile, his eyes, the backward tilt of his head, say this: "This is all too good to be true. Here is the realization of everything for which I've ever worked every day since high school, everything for which I've ever dared dream since I was a boy."

Mr. Brady, do I have this right? Is that what you were thinking just then?

JULY 27 / 9:30 P.M.
MYSTIC, CONNECTICUT

Likely because of a confluence of turning forty and becoming a father, I've become increasingly obsessed with watching football again. Perhaps it's psychological. And chemical. I'm probably compensating for having spent too much time walking around with a Baby Björn and now tending to a preschooler in pink footie pajamas. I've read about studies that show that men's testosterone levels decrease after having children. So perhaps I've turned to football to carve out a mildly macho bit of space.

Or maybe it's because I'm less and less enamored with my job. I could retire now. I never understand people who say they wouldn't know what they would do with their time. You give me a free morning, a walk, a cup of coffee, the newspaper, and it will be noon before I've even turned to the sports page.

For whatever reason, for the last couple of autumns I've become increasingly eager each week for the game. I get agitated if I can't watch it in peace. Last season, during every week leading up to Sunday, I found myself constantly looking at NFL.com and my team's website, sometimes a couple of times an hour. I've started to listen to sports radio. Even a couple of months ago, in May, I continued to check the websites and listen to the radio punditry, with the NFL draft over, when absolutely nothing was going on. And now with training camp started, I'm keeping tabs on every player and rumor and counting the days until the first regular-season game (forty-three).

My team, the New England Patriots, is the most successful football franchise of the last dozen years. Since the 2001–2 season, they've appeared in the Super Bowl five times and won three of them. They've won their division for ten of the last twelve years.

The quarterback during all of this recent success has been Thomas Edward Patrick Brady Jr. He's won more play-off games than any other quarterback in history. He's won the Super Bowl MVP twice. More recently, he has been the league MVP twice. The first time he earned the top individual honor, he had led his team to an unprecedented, undefeated regular season. The second time he was the league MVP, he was the only player in history ever voted the award unanimously. Tom Brady holds a few other all-time records, including the most touchdown passes in a season. If he holds pace this coming year, he'll also soon break the record for the most consecutive games in which a quarterback has thrown at least one touchdown.

The fact is that even if Tom Brady had stopped playing at

the age of twenty-eight, after just five years in pro football, he would've been a shoo-in for the Hall of Fame.

Yet despite all this glory, Tom Brady seems genuinely classy and modest when he's interviewed. He is square-jawed, cleft-chinned, and *GQ* handsome. When off the field, Tom Brady, like a twenty-first-century Joe Namath, often dresses in high-fashion, metrosexual outfits and always sports a new hairstyle or a new variation with his facial hair. He is married to one of the most beautiful and wealthiest supermodels in the world, Gisele Bündchen, who is also tall and dirty blond and off-the-charts successful. Gisele is Brazilian and has legs as tall as my neck. Brady and Bündchen are building a mansion on the ocean side of Beverly Hills, reportedly worth over $25 million. It has a moat. The couple have two little kids together and regularly care for a third from Brady's previous girlfriend, the Hollywood actress Bridget Moynahan.

Tom Brady is thirty-five years old. I'm forty-three.

As he gets ready for another season, I find myself frustrated and disappointed about how it's all pretty much turned out for me. I look back at so many mistakes, so many missed opportunities, so many times in my life that I wasn't the man I wish I could be. What I think would really help is a relaxed, genuine conversation with Tom Brady as we toss the ball back and forth. I have some things I really need to ask this man.

JULY 28 / 10:15 P.M.
MYSTIC, CONNECTICUT

My first break in trying to meet Brady came about a month ago when I got an interview with Seth Wickersham, a feature writer for *ESPN: The Magazine*. After reading his article on the quarterback in this summer's issue, I e-mailed the author. To my surprise he wrote right back, and then we spoke over the phone.

Seth has interviewed Brady three times. The first time was in 2001, right after he took over for the injured quarterback Drew Bledsoe. It was Brady's second year on the team, after being fourth string the previous year. Seth caught up with Brady a couple of months before he would go on to win that first Super Bowl, the night of The Photograph. At the time of their first interview, Seth himself was also in the second year of a new job. He and Brady both graduated college the same year, so Seth, who graduated from the University of Missouri, told me that he feels a certain kinship with Brady, who also went to a huge school, the University of Michigan. They're the same age, and both got their breaks at the same time. To set up that first interview, after Seth's initial contact with the team, Brady called him directly on the phone. The two met at the stadium, in some office-lounge. Brady wore sweatpants and either had a six-pack of beer in a backpack or was on his way to get one, as Seth remembers it, because he had lost a bet with a teammate over the Michigan vs. Michigan State game.

"I wouldn't say that we're friends," Seth told me, "but we're friendly. We've chatted at Super Bowl parties and so on."

"Has he always had that grace?" I asked. "I mean, he always seems to answer the press's questions with such composure, always stays calm, takes the high road, speaks humbly. Has he always been like that?"

"I think he has. Always really professional. The truth is," Seth laughed, "Brady hasn't said anything newsworthy in ten years."

Seth's second interview with Brady was after the quarterback had hit mega-stardom in 2004, after winning his second Super Bowl in three years. Brady, Seth said, has been the same each time in that he always gave him his full attention during the interview: he never checked his phone or spoke as if he was thinking about being somewhere else.

With the third and most recent interview this past summer,

which he titled "What More Could Tom Brady Want?," Seth focused his article on Brady's family life. Seth also has a little kid. I told him that I have a preschooler, too, and that was something that appealed to me in his story: trying to imagine superstar Tom Brady as a father of three young children. "Certainly this recent article was about me, too," Seth explained on the phone. He wrote about how Brady walks around with songs from kids' movies stuck in his head, and how if he starts daydreaming about football while he's with his family, his wife will remind him of his priorities. Seth said: "That part in the article about Gisele asking him 'Is this a Tommy day or a family day?'—or him trying to just get a kiss from his kid when his sons won't give him one, that's certainly true for me. That's every guy."

Seth told me he thought this father angle "humanized" the sports icon. Along with Brady's current quest to win another Super Bowl trophy, Seth wrote that the quarterback has the equal goal of trying "to raise balanced kids in an unbalanced celebrity world."

Mr. Brady, well, what more could *you want? Anything besides "One more Super Bowl would be nice"? As I run a short out pattern, choose one of these two deals with the devil: you can have one more definitive Super Bowl win this season, defining you almost inarguably as the most successful in the history of the game—or, option two, your skills completely tank this year, you get cut from the team, but you're guaranteed that none of your kids will grow up with a destructive inferiority complex? Which one do you choose?*

"I worry about Brady for these next few seasons," I said. "I mean, do you think he'll know when to quit? I don't want to watch him all beat up and over the hill like Favre."

Star quarterback Brett Favre retired from the Packers as a future first-ballot Hall of Famer, but came right back into the sport with an ugly battle with Green Bay management. He got traded to a new team and then traded again the next year. By then he seemed too old on the field, beaten up, bedraggled with his shirt half out, helmet knocked sideways, throwing dumb interceptions at the worst times, and being tangled off the field in a scandal where he allegedly sent photos of his penis to a sideline reporter. I don't want to see Brady like that. It would be like seeing a drunk, slurring old Sean Connery denied at the bar by a woman. I want Brady instead to go out like the Denver Broncos' John Elway, at the pinnacle, after winning two Super Bowls in a row.

"Well," Seth pointed out, "remember Favre had his last team, the Vikings, within one play of getting to the Super Bowl."

Seth compared Brady more to Peyton Manning, the other "aging" legend who is still playing out his final years in an effort to also win one more Super Bowl.

"But I know what you mean," Seth continued. "Peyton hasn't set any benchmarks like Brady has, who has said outright, 'I want to play until I'm forty.' I think Peyton will play quarterback until he can't do it anymore. Brady, well, he might—he just might embarrass himself in the end. And that's because Brady loves football so much and wants to play so much. Have you seen *The Brady Six* documentary?"

I admitted I hadn't, but promised I'd watch it that night. Which I did.

"In the film Brady is tearing up as he talks about that draft day—ten years earlier. He literally has tears in his eyes as he explains about those six other quarterbacks being picked above him. Even though not one of those guys went on to do much of anything in the NFL. But you have to be an extremist, to have that extreme drive, to feel that much pain so many years later, in order to be so great at something. You saw how hard Brady took that, being picked 199th overall, in the sixth round. I don't think he still uses this as a chip on his shoulder, but it shows how much he cares."

As we finished the call, Seth told me: "I don't want to discourage you, but he gets a lot of requests for interviews. I could give you Tom's e-mail, but he wouldn't write you back, of course. Your best bet is to contact Stacey James, the press guy for the Patriots."

I've tried. Ever since I spoke to Seth, I've been trying to write the letter to Pressman James. But I just can't seem to find the words that might entice Tom Brady to want to speak with me, let alone have a catch.

JULY 29 / 7:30 P.M.
MYSTIC, CONNECTICUT

One of the things so intriguing about this man is how he has somehow kept up his modest image—I don't know if it's real or expertly crafted—but he projects himself as an "I owe it all to Mom, aw, shucks" underdog, even while his football success, his classic good looks, and his taste for designer clothes have him crowned and presiding with his Victoria's Secret queen over a Camelot of the ultrarich celebrity elite. His cleft chin and square jaw actually look strikingly similar to the man in the modern Patriots logo, minus any Elvis leanings.

Thus Tom Brady *is* the New England Patriots of the modern era. He is the face and primary actor of arguably the most successful dynasty in the history of the National Football League. He is the Messiah for those diehard Patriots fans who claim devotion back when the team was named the Boston Patriots and suffered through some low years as the league's punching bag.

All that said, I sometimes want Tom Brady to be a little bit less of a company man. A few days ago he spoke to the press outside the stadium for the first time after summer break. About four dozen microphones, smart phones, digital recorders, video cameras, and digital cameras squeezed around every part of him. Reporters asked him about one of his star tight ends, Aaron Hernandez, who over the summer had been released by the team after he was arrested on charges of a mob-style execution of a man named Odin Lloyd.

I'm not sure what I wanted of Brady, but it wasn't this. Sometimes it's painful watching him be so polished. It felt odd to hear him talk about winning football games and "getting back to our jobs." He wouldn't answer how he felt when he first heard about the murder and the arrest. Brady knew not to respond to a question about how Hernandez "fit in" with everyone in the locker room. At any opening, Brady tried to paint the Patriots organization in the best light, to disassociate the team from Hernandez, and, certainly, not to insert himself or the team in any aspect of the trial or the investigation.

"Everyone really takes the lead from Coach Belichick and Mr. Kraft," Brady said. "I know they've commented on how they feel. I think we as players just try to follow their lead. Hopefully we can go out and do something that our community can really be proud of. That's the important thing. We've had such great examples over the years."

Brady's hair was freshly buzzed, as if for a new school year.

On camera, wearing a blue Patriots hooded sweatshirt, he looked even more tan than he did from afar on the field. He seemed especially tall and astoundingly relaxed as he looked down on all the reporters who crowded their microphones up to him and pressed their devices toward his mouth.

Brady listed a few famous Patriots and talked about how well they wore the jersey and how they were not only good on the field, but also active in the community. He mentioned the Boston Marathon bombing of the past spring as another awful thing that nobody wished had happened. Then he said in response to another question, "At some point we have to get back to the task at hand." He started talking about football and his job as a captain and a quarterback.

I watched this on the NFL network. As Brady deflected questions about the Hernandez murder charge, the network scrolled across the bottom of the screen Tom Brady's passing statistics, from both last season and over his career.

None of this felt right. Maybe Brady could've spent more time expressing his condolences to the family of the man who was murdered. Maybe he could've said something about how sad it was to know someone on your team who is accused of an act like this. Don't pretend that you never laughed with Aaron Hernandez. Maybe I want Tom Brady to let us see him a little heartsick or disgusted about the whole thing. Or maybe simply not know how to handle a teammate accused of first-degree murder. Maybe he could've said something like: "Hey, football is meaningless in comparison to something like this. I don't know what to say. I'm totally shook up about it."

Mr. Brady, what do you actually think about Hernandez and what he's been accused of? Is there a moment that the two of you shared that now resonates loudly? Some part of your world must suddenly be put into some level of doubt. Right?

JULY 30 / 10:45 P.M.
MYSTIC, CONNECTICUT
Today at the gas station a man pulled in across from me in a blue El Camino—that sedan with a truck bed that goes back to the 1960s. He had it tricked out with everything Patriots. Flying Elvis painted on one side, Pat Patriot on the other, and both incorporated into red flames licking back from the hood and headlights. Now here was a committed fan.

"How you feeling about this fall?" I asked, as if unfazed by his Patriots super-ride. I noticed a Tom Brady bobblehead on the dash.

He shook his head. "I don't know what it's going to be like without Welker."

Wes Welker had been Tom Brady's most productive receiver for the last six years and seems to be one of the quarterback's best friends on and off the field. The rival Denver Broncos lured Welker away as a free agent. Now Welker will catch passes from Peyton Manning.

"I hear you," I said to the guy as I checked the oil in my van. "And who knows even if Gronk is going to be healthy."

Rob Gronkowski is the Patriots' young, Frankenstein-like tight end. He's the Patriots' most dominant threat, Brady's favorite target in the end zone, and a total mismatch for any defense.

But Gronkowski can't seem to stay away from injuries recently: ankle, arm, back. He has been hurt at the end of the last two seasons, which might have made the difference of one Super Bowl win and another Super Bowl appearance— and now he might not even be ready to start this September.

"Sure is going to be tough on Tom this fall," the guy said.

AUGUST 1 / 8:30 P.M.
MYSTIC, CONNECTICUT

As summer training camp continues and the sportswriters analyze each and every Brady throw to each and every new receiver in practice, I'm transcribing interviews from a few weeks ago when I set up a sign at an outdoor mall called "Olde Mistick Village." My sign says: "What Would You Ask Tom Brady?"

Olde Mistick Village is our local tourist trap, an outdoor maze of shops by the highway. I wanted middle-aged men to relax and open up their hearts about how they are thinking about Tom Brady in relation to their own lives. My image of how this would work:

But lugging a couch or an easy chair around isn't practical, so I clipped the sign to a music stand. I brought two folding chairs. It was brutally muggy, in the nineties all day, so too hot for me to bring Ruby. I thought I would offer free water from a cooler to anyone who stopped to talk, but Lisa pointed out that they'd probably kick me out if I did this, since the mall is a commercial area. So I picked the shadiest place I could find to set up. I didn't wear anything Patriots, just a nice collared shirt and khaki pants. I tried to be as clean-cut and generally outgoing as I could manage without looking religious in any way. Writing in a legal pad, I put my digital recorder out in the open on my lap.

Despite the heat, a lot of people did stop to talk to me. No one sat down as I'd hoped, but many were willing to chat. Families. Senior citizens. Pairs of young women arm in arm. A guy covered in tattoos. My friend Hoss came by and sat with me for a bit, which helped my courage.

Two boys who were about thirteen years old took me the most seriously. They stood and thought hard, whispered back and forth to each other, and even asked how many questions they were allowed.

"As many as you want," I said.

The two stood and listened as I spoke to others. Finally, their earnestness turned to sadness and then frustration.

"I just do not know," one of the boys said.

"What *would* I ask Tom Brady?" the other said to the sky.

Sullen and defeated, they walked away. I apologized. I encouraged them to come back later if they thought of something, anything.

Maybe one in thirty people hadn't heard of Tom Brady. One in three, I assume, thought I was trying to sell them something. One young woman who was actually wearing a Tom Brady jersey, for example, wouldn't stop to talk to me. I can sympathize, though, because if anybody asks me anything in a public place, I say "No, thank you," and keep going. I can barely take a free sample at a grocery store without feeling suspicious.

On the whole for this outing, the mall pedestrians' questions—which often shaped up to be more advice for the quarterback—fell into three rough categories. Here is an example for each, with a grab bag at the end:

1. *How long are you going to play, and how can you win another Super Bowl?*
   A woman in her fifties with a southern accent: "How many more years is he going to work? If he's in good shape, and he doesn't have any injuries, go for it. Make sure he's going to have a life after. Too many people get injuries, and they feel like shit the rest of their life. I don't think the career's worth it. If he's made good money, provided for his family—like myself, I do physical therapy work in a hospital. Been there fifteen years, and I'm like 'My God!' I'm only going to be fifty-six. Am I going to be doing this for the rest of my life? My boyfriend does pest control. Maybe I should join him killing bugs."

2. *What do you and Gisele do with all your money?*
   One of two older women walking together: "I would ask him to donate to the poor. What's his salary? All right then, he should donate eight million a year. I'd like to see him doing some community service then. To see what other people are doing that don't have that kind of money. Which is most of us, right? And not donate to the poor, like cars and stuff, but food. Next-door neighbors, Americans, have lost their jobs, and are without food. The only reason we stopped here now is because there was an accident on the highway. I bet Tom Brady doesn't sit in traffic."

3. *How is the offense going to be this season without all your receivers?*
   A man in his thirties with a white T-shirt with the sleeves cut off: "Brady is the heart [pronounced with a

Boston accent: *hah-t*] and soul of the team. He didn't take the increase, didn't ask for a lot of money, but Welker did. Very disappointed in Wes. He should've had the same attitude as Tom. I think Wes is looking at it as more of a business. Tom thinks of it as his career, his home, the place that gave him—made him what he is. I mean, who heard of Wes Welker before he got to the Patriots?" (This summer Brady took an extended contract with the Patriots until he is forty, which reduces his annual salary. This presumably was to make room within the Patriots' cap space—their league-mandated annual salary budget—for the team to pay Wes Welker more. But the receiver didn't stay.) As this guy left, I said: "Go Pats." He said: "One more ring, baby."

4. *Grab Bag*

A landscaper in his twenties: "Why does he keep choking in the playoffs in the last couple years?"

A woman in her forties, a New York Giants fan: "Why does he sit on the field and pout after he loses? See, look, I have that picture of him on my phone, sitting on the turf after he lost the second Super Bowl to us."

An older man dressed like a golfer: "Does he wish his wife wasn't so outspoken?" (This references the same Super Bowl loss. Immediately after the game a fan caught Gisele on video, which went viral. Gisele was talking to another player's wife and responding to some hecklers shouting at her about how the Giants quarterback is better. Gisele said: "My husband cannot fucking throw the ball and catch the ball at the same time." Then she drank furiously from her bottle of springwater.)

A father in his fifties, a Baltimore Ravens fan: "There's nothing I can ask Brady with language that's suitable in front of the children here." His wife said: "Why does he wear those ridiculous boots?" (These would be boots made by UGG, one of the few brands for which Brady advertises.)

One in a group of three women, laughing, maybe arriving in town for a bachelorette party: "Ask him if he waxes his back."

My setup at the mall was more successful than I expected and gave me a reason to talk to people I never would have. When my friend Hoss came, he asked me why I even care about professional football in the first place. Hoss is a science teacher with thick muttonchop sideburns, and he doesn't understand why anyone would spend a nice Sunday afternoon sitting inside and watching television, watching other people play some game. I explained that one reason I like pro football is that, like the weather, it's a safe, easy thing to talk about. Whenever I see my neighbor Matt, for example, walking his dog while I'm working in my backyard, we launch right into a discussion of the Patriots and our pleasure in seeing the New York Jets degrade. I don't even know what Matt does for a living.

One surprising thing that happened as I was collecting questions for Brady was that I found myself lying. One large alluring falsehood slipped right out of my mouth without premeditation or resistance. I had spent a lot of time making the sign and considering what I should wear, but I hadn't planned on how to answer exactly *why* I was sitting there soliciting questions for the superstar.

"I'm a writer," I started answering. Then I lied: "I'm going to be meeting Tom Brady soon. I'm collecting questions from The People, from regular people off the street."

Did someone record me on his or her phone? It's probably already on YouTube, which means one of Brady's people has by now entered me into the crazy person database. My friend Lenny suggested I set up a Facebook page or start a blog to try to find Brady's biggest fan and collect what all the people in the world want to ask the quarterback. Though I'd be fascinated to hear from some Icelandic or Vietnamese or even Boston football fan, I do not want to have an online presence about my mission. I want to have a real conversation with Brady, and my assumption is that if you're a mega-celebrity you have some kind of e-mail list for when you have become the focus of a crazy person. Your agent or personal assistant zaps an e-mail message out to all the people the annoyance is likely to contact—close family, friends, teammates—and it says: "Please do not grant interviews to [fill in name of crazy person]."

Mr. Brady, is it indeed someone's job each day to search for people pursuing your attention? If so, how many crazies do you have to worry about each year? And does this member of your staff try to identify the motives of said crazies, and then hem them in legally and logistically? Does this member of your staff update you monthly on new or especially persistent crazies? Weekly?

AUGUST 2 / 9:30 P.M.
MYSTIC, CONNECTICUT

I've considered various covert strategies and methods of disguise to meet the man, such as posing as one of his landscapers or slipping in as one of his golf caddies, but in the end I haven't come up with anything viable. The security around him must be huge, and, again, those methods wouldn't get me the kind of audience I want. I'm not going to try to contact

Gisele or any of his family. Thus the direct honest approach as a writer, even though I'm not a sports journalist, seems my best option.

To get myself centered, I've bought a gray sweatshirt hoodie and cut off the sleeves below the elbow. I'm wearing it now with the hood over my head, with a dour expression, to look like Coach Bill Belichick. This is the garb that the Patriots coach—by far the most successful coach active today—usually wears on the sideline. He and Brady together have the highest winning percentage and have won by far more games than any other coach-quarterback tandem in NFL history since the NFL-AFL merger. The Denver Broncos are the only team that does not have a career losing record against Brady and Belichick, and they are merely tied. All this is still more impressive since they began their partnership after the introduction of free agency and the salary cap, which in

an effort toward league parity allows good players to be lured elsewhere and makes it nearly impossible for teams to retain the same talented guys season after season. A rich owner, for example, can no longer buy up all the best players and keep them.

Notoriously, even comically, Belichick speaks to reporters in monotone, without irony, in an overt effort to hoard even the slightest scrap of information that might be useful to an upcoming opponent. During press conferences, he grips the podium uncomfortably, wearing his sweatshirt. His treatment of reporters is often condescending. At these press conferences Coach Belichick is the perfect foil to well-spoken, polite, impeccably dressed Brady. While his lead disciple Tom Brady is like Luke Skywalker, Bill Belichick is like a terse, humorless Ben Kenobi—or, if you hate the Patriots, Darth Vader.

As I continue to struggle with my draft of an opening letter to Pressman Stacey James, I've been trucking along with other correspondence and logistics for the upcoming months. Yesterday I wrote to Peter King, the preeminent writer for *Sports Illustrated*, who interviews Brady regularly. I wrote to Charles Pierce, author of an early biography of Brady. I tried to buy tickets to the Patriots-Broncos game in November by starting twenty minutes before sale time and constantly hitting refresh on two computers while redialing on a phone. The screen ticked to "sold out" instantly, as soon as the clock turned to the opening minute.

I did get one huge lead from a colleague: the president of the Patriots, Jonathan Kraft, is both an alumnus and a trustee of the college in Massachusetts for which I teach. I wrote to the dean of faculty to see if he could help me contact Mr. Kraft.

All this is starting to consume quite a bit of time. My job is as a literature professor. I teach "Literature of the Sea." But I'm more of a third-string instructor at an off-campus program. If you know anything about academia and the ivory tower, you know this mission to meet Tom Brady is one gargantuan procrastination and not even mildly what I'm supposed to be doing if I want to advance my career. My wife, who for her part is a first-string science professor, works fulltime, too. And we have our daughter. And the house to clean. And the lawn to mow. The hedge to trim. (Quietly judgmental neighbors surround us.) And the van to fix yet again. And

Ruby keeps getting out from some unknown hole in the fence that I can't find. She'll sometimes spend an hour or more in the patch of woods behind our house or prowling through our neighbors' yards. I can usually hear her in the brush, or catch a flash of her brown fur, but once she gets the scent of our local feral cats, she won't listen to anybody. And our back deck looks awful because last year I thought white primer was a good idea under green deck paint, so now after months of Alice tricycling in circles, the porch looks like it's been dive-bombed by a landfill's worth of seagulls.

Meanwhile, Brady and his teammates are lifting weights, doing drills, scrimmaging, watching film, and studying the playbook. Brady is meeting with his personal coaches to analyze his conditioning and throwing motion with the highest available technology and expertise.

Mr. Brady, maybe this is obvious, but you do have a full-time nanny, yes? Do you ever feel like you spend a half hour of every day trying to find the other yellow sock with the sunflower design so you can get out the door with your child? Do you feel odd when you walk out of your house and there's someone hired to mow your lawn? Do you and Gisele each have a personal assistant? If so, do these two assistants meet each day? Do the two of them meet with the nanny apart from you—while someone is making you breakfast? Would you explain to me how it all works in your house on a normal day of preseason? Do you write your own checks? Do you drive your own car? Does Gisele correct you when you improperly load the dishwasher so that the little Tupperwares flip upside down and fill up with water or get whipped to the bottom then melted? Do you mind that Gisele reportedly makes about $42 million a year and you make only $38 million?

I interviewed Matt Cassel today! As per the arrangement we set up, the Minnesota Vikings public-relations guy called me first. On my office phone's screen it read "Minnesota Vikings." The pressman told me to wait. Then a minute later the phone rang again.

"Hi, this is Matt Cassel."

Matt has a deep voice and seemed very Californian, very laid back.

"Thanks so much for taking this time, I really appreciate it," I said. "I don't expect you to necessarily open up to me in twenty minutes—but basically, um, well, I'm trying to understand a little bit more about what life is like for you. Because for most middle-aged guys that I know, being an NFL quarterback is absolutely the coolest thing we could ever imagine. Could I start with what you think the average American doesn't understand about the life of a quarterback?"

Matt Cassel is a curious case. He played quarterback in college at football powerhouse USC, yet never earned the starting spot. He was beat out each year by a starter who went on to win the Heisman Trophy, which is college football's highest individual honor. Cassel, as well as most everyone else, didn't think he'd ever make it in the NFL, since he never started a college game. But the Patriots saw something in him, and they drafted the backup in a basement round.

Cassel remained a backup quarterback for the Patriots for his first three years in the league, then had a breakout season for the team when Brady got hurt in 2008. Cassel played so well that season that he earned a huge contract and the starting job with the Kansas City Chiefs. This went okay for a couple of years, but then the Chiefs went downhill, and Cassel took much of the blame. Now this preseason he's beginning training camp for a third team, the Minnesota Vikings. He comes in as the new backup behind a younger quarterback whose own job as the starter is under question.

Cassel told me that most people don't recognize that football players are just like they are. "We're just the lucky 1 percent of the 1 percent to make it in this sport," he said.

This, I didn't point out to him, makes him exactly *not* like the rest of us.

"At the end of the day, y'know, it's funny," he said. "We're sitting around here after practice at training camp, and you look around and realize that we're all just normal people. People think it's glamorous, but I care about the same things." He spoke about his family and about enjoying taking his girls to the pool during the off-season.

"What was it like playing with Brady?" I asked.

"He was my mentor, and had . . . *has* such a tremendous impact. We still play golf. He's a great friend of mine. Dear friend of mine. We still work out together in the off-season, but our relationship is now well beyond football. We talk football when we see each other, but that's not all of it. There's a camaraderie to the game. My best friends are guys I've played football with, because they've shared that same experience."

Cassel told me how Brady inspired him when he was at his first NFL training camp in 2005, helped him make the team, and then regularly earn the spot as his backup.

Everything changed, though, again, in the first quarter of the first regular season game in 2008, which, ironically, was against the Chiefs. An opposing defender tackled Brady low, right after he threw the ball deep downfield to Randy Moss. The hit bent Brady's left knee awkwardly as he stepped forward with that leg to throw, tearing his anterior cruciate ligament, better known as his ACL. With his arm around a trainer, Brady limped off the field and hobbled down to the locker room.

"I had gotten to play a lot during preseason that year, which was great," Cassel said. "But for that first game of the season I was personally a bit more relaxed, settling in to watch Tom work. The pass down the sideline that went up to Randy Moss, I was watching the ball, which ended up in a turnover. So I didn't see Tom until I realized he didn't get up. Tom is one of the toughest guys I've ever met. No matter how hard he's hit, he's going to get up, so when he didn't, I knew he was hurt really badly. I thought to myself, I mean, all that mix of emotions. Nervous butterflies. I had better find my helmet! The Chiefs had the ball because of the turnover, and within minutes the doctor came up to me before I even went on the field and said 'Tom's done for the season. It's your team now.'"

At that point Brady was the reigning league MVP from the Patriots' preceding nearly perfect season, the field general for what remains the highest single-season scoring offense in the history of the NFL. At that opening game, Brady was third in league history for consecutive starts by a quarterback.

"So I had all kinds of emotions," Cassel said. "And then, I'll never forget, as I'm running out onto the field, and we're pinned down near our own end zone, all of the fans in New England gave me a standing ovation. A couple plays went by, and then Randy was supposed to run a deeper slant, but he threw his hand up, so I threw the ball long and he went up and got it. After that sixty-yard play, that calmed my nerves. It wasn't until after the game that I realized the full weight of the situation. It dawned on me. Here I was now, front and center. I stood up on the stand for my first press conference."

I was surprised at how easy and collegial our conversation flowed. He told me about the rest of that season and expressed how difficult it became for his family when he went to Kansas City and then took the brunt from the fans when the team was losing. He pointed out that the quarterback is the only position that touches, distributes the ball on every play. He's the most important position on the field, but he also gets too much of the credit and too much of the blame.

"Do you sometimes look at the crowd," I said, "at all of the people in the stands during the season, or even now at training camp, and wonder just what they're doing? I mean, why they're there?"

He recognized how much of an impact football can make, how important it is to people. "Here in Minnesota, every single night of training camp, at nine, ten at night, we come out of meetings and there are little kids—three, four years old—with their families waiting to get an autograph."

Before we hung up I wished him luck for the season, and thanked him perhaps too much. It did feel, though, as if he would've talked with me for longer. I wanted to ask his advice about how I should go about getting an interview with Brady, but that felt rude.

Maybe getting to speak to Brady isn't going to be that hard after all?

AUGUST 5 / 10:30 P.M.
MYSTIC, CONNECTICUT

The dean of faculty wrote a kind e-mail back about helping me contact the president of the Patriots: "I do know Jonathan—he is an active trustee, and many of us know him fairly well." But, he said, this sort of contact with a trustee should really go through another office at the college, so he sent my request along to the administrator there.

That contact aside, the truth is that if I have any hopes of speaking to Brady *before* the regular season starts, while he has more time and presumably more patience for something like this, I need to write to the Patriots press office immediately—to Pressman James. It's less than a week until the first preseason game and then four more weeks until the regular season.

Here's a draft of my e-mail (or should I begin with a paper letter?):

Dear Mr. James:
I have begun a self-reflective study of middle-aged masculine mediocrity, football, and celebrity in America today. I wonder if it might be at all possible to schedule an interview with Tom Brady at his convenience? I am sure he is exceptionally busy and has many requests for his time, but I hope this will be a different kind of discussion. Perhaps we could even have a catch? I'm not a sports journalist or a fashion writer. I have candidly little to offer him in return, but I have, once, in a fury of midlife crisis energy, sailed solo across the Atlantic in a 28-foot sailboat. It's perhaps the most interesting thing about me, and might be a curiosity for Mr. Brady? (I also own a Volkswagen minibus, which I read that his family had when he was growing up.)
Thank you so very much for considering this and passing my request for an interview along to Mr. Brady. I would be happy to explain more about my project over e-mail or on the phone.
Sincerely,
Richard King, PhD

Oh, Jeez. This will not do. This is bearing down on hopeless.

AUGUST 8 / 10:15 P.M.
MYSTIC, CONNECTICUT

I got a prompt and encouraging e-mail today from an administrator at the college. She wrote:

Thanks for reaching out. I checked with Mr. Kraft's team, and they explained that they direct all inquiries of this nature to their media relations colleagues. They shared this number for you to use [and she gave me the number]. Best of luck with this endeavor.

Okay, I thought. All right. Not exactly the red carpet, but at least they gave me the phone number to his office. I set myself up by the phone, hooked up my audio recorder, and unwrapped a fresh notepad. I tested two pens. I took a few deep breaths. I dialed.

My plan was to ask for an interview with Jonathan Kraft, ideally to come up to Foxborough and meet with him in person. I'd tell his secretary that I wanted to talk to Mr. Kraft about himself, his remembrances of his time in college, about his success in business, about being a middle-aged man—he's forty-nine—and then, if he had time, to discuss his experiences and thoughts about Mr. Brady. Jonathan Kraft is a short Jewish man like me, so I was not above pulling this card, too. "Shalom, Mr. Kraft!"

The phone rang three times. Then: "You have reached the Patriots media relations department. No one is available to accept your call at this time. Please leave your name, number, person you are calling for, and the time of day that you called. . . ."

I put down the phone quietly as it beeped for a message.

AUGUST 10 / 1:15 A.M.
EN ROUTE FROM PHILADELPHIA
BACK TO MYSTIC, CONNECTICUT

Inside the van at a rest stop on the New Jersey Turnpike. I've got the passenger seat swiveled backwards—one of my favorite features of the vw camper—so that I have the swing table turned to my right side, and a coffee milkshake at the ready. Doing a little writing here in my journal before I get back on the road.

I'm on the way home after watching the Patriots' first pre-season game of the year with my oldest friend, Dave, whom we always call "Dumptruck." Through his friend at work, he got some cheap end-zone tickets. This was the first live professional sports event I've seen in literally more than *twenty years*. Which to calculate makes me feel like I'm coughing cobwebs.

I should get one thing off my chest here. I have not been a lifelong Patriots fan. And though I grew up outside Philadelphia, I wasn't always primarily a Philadelphia Eagles fan. As a kid I latched onto the Pittsburgh Steelers. This was in the late 1970s, when quarterback Terry Bradshaw and silky receiver Lynn Swann led this Steelers team to four Super Bowl victories in six years. Pittsburgh dominated with the "Steel Curtain" defensive line: L. C. Greenwood, Dwight White, Ernie Holmes, and my favorite player then, number seventy-five, "Mean Joe" Greene. In 1976 their defense recorded three shutout games in a row, something unfathomable in today's NFL. I still have my collection of eleven Mean Joe Greene All-Pro trading cards. Still smells like gum.

The truth is that I've always been a fair-weather fan. I'm not proud of this, but I like to follow a winner. I've come to realize, to try to accept about myself, that I want to feel good at the end of a Sunday. I mean, I did start following the Patriots after I settled in Connecticut some fifteen years ago, but I'd be lying if I didn't admit that their regular dominance in the Brady era has kept me involved. That's another thing about following sports that I've been trying to explain to Hoss. Spectator sports give fans a chance to feel good about something, even a little successful, as if we have absolutely anything to do with a given win. We have given the team our vote. We've invested in them with our time, finances, and emotions. As I disappoint myself all week long, at least Tom Brady is there on Sunday to do well, which somehow makes me feel better.

Anyway, it was such a fine thing tonight to sit with my oldest friend with a beer and a hoagie and watch live football. When Dumptruck and I were in elementary school and even into middle school, we would watch *NFL Films* on Sunday morning TV and then run down to the park and play one-on-one. We pulled on jerseys and wrapped up our hands and forearms with ace bandages as if we were linemen all taped up like Mean Joe Greene. We played in mud and snow and knocked the snot out of each other until we collapsed on the ground out of exhaustion. On days we weren't playing, we traced quarters on construction paper and made them into football helmets, like this:

I played organized football in middle school, but Dumptruck's mom wouldn't let him, and then neither of our mothers let us play football in high school. "You're going to get paralyzed," my mother said.

The Patriots-Eagles game tonight, even though it is preseason, was far more of a production than I anticipated. We watched fireworks at multiple occasions, spouts of smoke, cheerleaders, a drum squad, a male flag-waving troupe and their bald-eagle mascot "Swoop," hopping and leaping on the sidelines. I was most surprised by the volume and pervasiveness of music. Between every break in the action, presumably commercial breaks, the stadium cranked music—hip-hop, rock, and heavy metal. They played the *Rocky* theme song. No matter what was playing, people around us stood up and danced. This was not the sporting event of my dad and uncles, or even what I remembered vaguely from the couple of games I'd gone to as a kid.

As cameramen panned the crowd, people were caught on the massive television screens waving and dancing and lunging themselves toward the camera. It's one of those things we never seem to tire of. They should try this for people waiting at the department of motor vehicles.

And those video screens! There's simply no way *not* to watch the screens. Lincoln Financial Field in Philadelphia has two massive Jumbotrons, one at each end of the field. It turns out that the Philly screens at ninety-six by twenty-seven feet are actually about average, if not on the smaller side, compared to half the other teams' Jumbotrons. Even during the game, during any given play, I had to concentrate to watch the field and *not* to stare up at the screen.

Author Charles Pierce wrote about how modern football on television has singled out players as individuals in a new way. "The quarterback is central to the television program that is the average NFL game," Pierce wrote. "The camera loves him, follows him everywhere, even to the sideline." The pro athlete these days is also ex officio a media personality. This is the only profession within the entertainment field where someone enters the public eye as a secondary purpose, regardless of the athlete's desire for the attention. Unlike the screen or the stage, the audience is not, theoretically, the athlete's primary concern. Yet the quarterback in football, more than any other sport, is inevitably the lead singer of the band, the Broadway star, and the leading man in the Hollywood blockbuster.

Much of this is true even in the stadium, where on these big screens you see close-ups of the men's faces, rather than just the helmets, pads, and numbers running around in the distance. The Jumbotrons try, backwardly, to make it feel like you're at home watching TV. During halftime Dumptruck and I watched dogs catch Frisbees on the field—on the Jumbotron.

Tonight Coach Belichick took Brady out of the game a few minutes into the second quarter, to give the backups playing time and to make sure the superstar didn't get injured. Brady had scored touchdowns on both of his drives. The Patriots offense ran the ball in huge chunks, and Brady surgically, methodically, carved up the Eagles defense, completing every single pass, aside from one he threw away to avoid a sack.

Tom Brady is now the oldest player on the team. He and nose tackle Vince Wilfork are the only remaining Patriots from their last Super Bowl win almost ten years ago (which was Wilfork's rookie year). And indicative of the turnover in the league today, Brady, Wilfork, and offensive lineman Logan Mankins are the only three players remaining from the Patriots team that went undefeated in the regular season —only five years ago. Until Gronk comes back, Julian Edelman is Brady's *only* healthy starting receiver from last year, and Edelman—also injured last year for about half the season—has perennially been a backup since he arrived on the team. Edelman only caught twenty-one passes last season.

With a new cast, Tom Brady seems to be beginning all over again for one last run for it all.

Dumptruck and I spent a good deal of time discussing grown men and women wearing football jerseys. First of all, an authentic NFL jersey will set you back $100—and if you want an "elite" jersey with all the high-tech fabrics that the players wear, that goes for $250. Some people pay still more to have their own name stitched on the back, but most fans have their favorite player's name. Rough guess, maybe one in ten people at the stadium tonight wore an Eagles or Patriots jersey. They represented a variety of eras, so that if you know the history of a team or the continually rotating roster, there's a nod of recognition, even a few exchanges between strangers as they walk around buying food and drinks. Like this:

"Hey, Randall Cunningham! Vintage."

"Hey, thanks, buddy. Nice work yourself on the Steve Grogan."

Or if a guy sees another man wearing the exact same jersey, say a white Patriots Wes Welker number eighty-three, there's either a glance away as two people might react when noticing they're wearing the same sweater at a party, or instead a pride in mutual good taste acknowledged with a nod, a fist bump, or a quip like this: "There you go, Wes!"

"Yeah, hey! Wish he were here tonight, right?"

"I hope he does well up there in Denver —"

"But that the Broncos and Peyton suck it, right?"

I wore my Pat Patriot hat proudly, but I'm not at the jersey stage yet. I'd be too embarrassed walking around wearing a football jersey with a player's name on it, even at the game itself. This is partly because I would feel like too much of a *spectator*, which has a listless, passive, almost defeatist connotation for me. I know, I know, I'm well aware of the irony of this belief. I'm aware that within my mission to meet Tom Brady I'm a hairball of hypocrisy. But wearing a jersey, if you're a guy, it practically says *I wish I were this man.* And if you're a woman wearing a football player's jersey, it's almost like saying *I want to have sex with him.*

Dumptruck called me out on that one. "That's not true. There are plenty of women who know more than us about football. They can be into a player just as a fan." (As I write now, actually, walking back toward her car at this rest stop is a woman wearing a Patriots Jerod Mayo jersey, number fifty-one, the team's best linebacker.)

Dumptruck did concede that he wouldn't wear a jersey around, either. We talked about how it reminded us of high school when we played lacrosse together (our mothers let us play this sport). On game day it was the custom to wear our lacrosse uniforms in school. If you had a girlfriend—which neither of us ever had in high school—she might be the one to wear your jersey to classes that day.

As I drifted from the Eagles to the Steelers as a kid, then largely forgot about professional football until returning to the game full bore in recent years as a Patriots fan, Dumptruck has remained faithful to the Eagles. But I was still surprised to hear him stand up every once in a while to shout out "There you go!" or "C'mon!" He often celebrated a first down by launching up and delivering a full-body karate chop toward the opposing end zone. For my part I just sat and clapped whenever something good happened with the Patriots. Did I even stand up once, tonight?

Dumptruck and his wife have three little kids. He's a smart guy, a history major in college, but he never seemed to have any broader aspirations beyond working as a landscaper and a mason. At the end of a given day, I've sent several dozen e-mails and graded a pile of undergraduate essays on Joseph Conrad or Kate Chopin, while he has created something useful with his hands, outside, and made something tangibly, visibly better. I told him about how my hands are soft now, ever since I stopped working on ships, and how what I think I'd really like to be doing, my pipe dream, is a little business where I repair and finish small boats in my backyard. The smell of sawdust, my own schedule, the dog snuffling around. I see guys living that life all over my town.

Dumptruck listened and agreed and took me seriously. Because that's the kind of person he is. He would be a gifted priest. As Dumptruck has been getting older and the expenses of his family pile up, he's been looking for jobs that are easier on his body, pay better, and offer more security.

I asked him in the fourth quarter: "How's the midlife crisis going?"

"All fine," he smiled. "I think the wife has had a few for me, so I'm covered by now. How's yours?"

I told him about this whole Tom Brady thing. I asked him what he would ask the quarterback if he thought he could get a real answer.

Dumptruck said: "Prove to me you're not a cyborg."

Mr. Brady, can you prove to my oldest friend that you're not a cyborg?

AUGUST 13 / 2:30 P.M.
HANOVER, NEW HAMPSHIRE

Our vacation is not going well. We're camping in the rain and just finished driving around for an hour to get Alice to nap.

To get ready for this trip a couple of weeks ago we put a bunch of money into the van to fix it up again for family travel. I had a new radio with a CD player installed and had the shop fix the AC, the starter, the horn, the speedometer, the driver-side power window, and a few other things.

The mechanic said: "And I fixed the muffler. Some other guy put it in backwards."

"That would be me," I said.

He tried to give me an out about how easy it is to mix up. It isn't.

A week later, while I was driving home from visiting my uncle Frank—who, by the way, loves my mission to meet

Brady—the gas pedal separated from the floor. It had rusted out. I was by myself and able to limp home with a plastic cable-tie jury-rig. At the house I fixed the pedal with fiberglass and some stainless screws, and I was feeling pretty good about the repair and ready to roll on our camping trip. Lisa and I packed up that morning, checked everything off our list, got Alice and Ruby in the van, and pulled out of the driveway with a carefree double-beep of the newly rewired horn.

When we turned up onto the highway ten minutes later, the van could not get into third gear. I had been ignoring some indications of this recently, but it hadn't done anything like this. I was hoping it might just go away?

We drove slowly back home, ditching most of our gear back inside the house, and packed only the essentials up to the roof of our little old hatchback. Only Ruby was happy, because she got to be on a sleeping bag right next to Alice.

The silver lining is that the van broke down right away, not when we were trying to get up over the mountains of New Hampshire. But I think it's going to be the last straw for Lisa. I can't blame her. Man, I don't want to say good-bye to this ride. We bought the van to drive cross-country, before we had Alice about five years ago. Lisa, Ruby, and I drove the slow lane the whole way and camped from Connecticut to Puget Sound, then down south to LA, and back across the country via the southern route. Despite several sketchy performances and a thousand dollars here and there over the years, the van has always delivered. Well, that's not entirely true, either. Oh, dear old van. I've cared for you the best I could, but there seems to always be something new that goes wrong. I don't have the time or expertise to keep you running. I wish I were retired and could tinker and learn all day long. It's not like I can just throw money at the problem either. Even the vw mechanics don't know what will go wrong next. Faith, earnestness, and even a bankroll can't make this thing thrive again.

Things are going better now that we're no longer camping, and we're with friends who also have young kids.

I checked the Web on Jim's computer, and there was a report that Brady hurt his knee in a joint practice with the Tampa Bay Buccaneers. This proved a false alarm, but not before releasing a twenty-four-hour gush of emotion across the sporting world. A shaky amateur video clip taken from the stands went viral, as the man says "Oooh, no!" with all the pathos and horror of someone realizing the ramifications of this particular star quarterback falling down on the grass clutching his surgically repaired left knee. Brady was back playing the next day. Patriots fans recommenced breathing. And number twelve returned to wearing his knee brace.

Jim took his two kids and me on a ride yesterday afternoon, powering his motorboat down Somes Sound. Jim and I held on and shouted over the engine. More than any other middle-aged man so far, he understands my need to have a catch and a conversation with Brady.

"What's Lisa think about it?" he asked, shouting into my ear away from his kids.

"The truth is, I'm not really sure. She's always been good about my shenanigans, and she's been supportive of letting me plan a bunch of short trips so far. I guess I think she does want me to get to meet him, if that's what I really want. But she's not that into football."

"Does she watch with you?"

"Every once in a while. She's one of those people that will cheer for a good play, regardless if it's the Patriots or not."

"Ooo. That's hard. Ann does that, too. Or she'll ask you about some rule—"

"—that makes you realize that you don't actually know the rule yourself—"

"—but never even thought to wonder about it! Exactly. Well, maybe Lisa figures it's better than you having some affair. Or buying a red Corvette convertible."

"She'd probably prefer the convertible to our van right now."

As we motored along, Jim pointed out all the mansions on the sound. The owners spend only a few days a year in these sprawling palaces. I told him about the $25 million house that Brady and Gisele are finishing in Southern California. Overhead photographs have surfaced, and there will be an entire cover feature about the mansion in *Architectural Digest* this fall. Their house is nearly fourteen thousand square feet and has a swimming pool with a vanishing edge so that it appears from the house as if it empties into the Pacific Ocean itself.

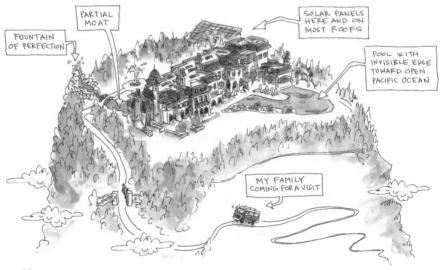

Reportedly the Bündchen-Brady "eco-chic" Mount Olympus also has a variety of environmental features, including solar panels, composting toilets, a garden, and a chicken coop. It's constructed with environmentally friendly or reclaimed materials. This is laudable, I suppose, but if you're building something that large for one family, consuming that much space and material and plumbing and electricity and labor and shipping, it wouldn't matter if it were made out of organic grasses and native beeswax.

This summer the power couple also bought a $135,000 Lexus. News reports say it's a hybrid. That it has environmentally friendly wood paneling inside.

Certainly the media reports might be exaggerated, and surely the couple has not the time nor the interest in correcting inaccuracies in these sorts of stories. But still. As she jets all over the world, Gisele likes to give talks about global climate change and environmental responsibility as a "goodwill ambassador" for the United Nations Environment Programme.

Mr. Brady, you two share a private plane, yes? Is it your perception that, as public figures, you and Gisele strike a balance between living a high-consumption lifestyle and setting an example for The People? Or do you see yourself less as an ambassador like Gisele, but more simply as a football player, whose job is not to be a role model? Do you sometimes look at the choices you've made, where you are now, and wonder why you're not living the lifestyle you claim you believe in?

"What would I ask Tom Brady?" Jim said as he throttled the engine down. We floated in a little cove to let the kids peer over the rail to try to spot a lobster. "His success stems from his motivation, right? I'm curious how someone as successful as Brady motivates himself. Is it inherent? Or does he consciously work at it?"

Jim continued: "Then I've got a bunch of secondary questions about his work habits. Does he have a specific and detailed daily schedule, even during the off-season? Are there times when he just doesn't feel like working? What does he envision doing after football, and does he think it'll be hard to maintain the same level of discipline and commitment? It's all self-serving, because I'm curious how someone like him excels at something, because I feel like I have potential but never really excelled the way I—maybe—I could have."

He lowered his voice away from the kids.

"That sounds more negative than I want, a maudlin forty-nine-year-old. I'm really satisfied with my life, particularly my family life, but I do feel I've maybe not achieved professionally as much as I could. Does it sound like I'd be asking Tom for a therapy session?"

AUGUST 19 / 10:15 P.M.
ROCKLAND, MAINE

I got a haircut at the local barber and asked him if he'd make me look like Tom Brady.

The other barber leaned over and said, "Which of his haircuts you want?"

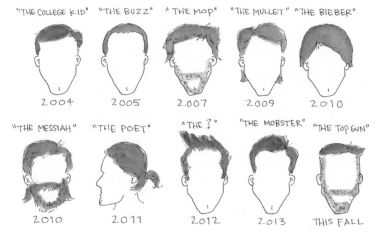

"THE COLLEGE KID"   "THE BUZZ"   "THE MOP"   "THE MULLET"   "THE BIEBER"
2004   2005   2007   2009   2010

"THE MESSIAH"   "THE POET"   "THE ?"   "THE MOBSTER"   "THE TOP GUN"
2010   2011   2012   2013   THIS FALL

So commenced a conversation between two Maine barbers and me about the progression of Brady's hairstyles and facial hair over the years.

Objectively, I think the fighter-pilot-style haircut he gave me, with just a little left on top and in front, does indeed make me look a bit more like Brady. He often sports a five o'clock shadow, which I don't think works so well for me. Just so long as he doesn't grow a beard again. That hasn't worked for a quarterback since Dan Fouts and Kenny Stabler wore them (and still won games) in the early '80s.

AUGUST 24 / 10 P.M.
MYSTIC, CONNECTICUT

Maybe I'm not getting enough exercise. I used to run and bike all the time. In my twenties I ran the Boston Marathon and a couple of other endurance races. But more recently, once Alice came along, I got so much busier. So that when I do have free time I use it to prepare classes and mark papers (and watch football) instead of getting outdoors. Last week a friend gave us his old jogging stroller, and I excavated two objects from deep in my closet. So long forgotten, I had to bring in an anthropologist friend for identification.

Alice wakes up at 5:15 no matter what time she goes to bed at night. We're all used to the schedule by now, so I love this time with her. While Lisa gets a bit more sleep, Alice, Ruby, and I go for a walk every morning to get a bagel for her and a coffee for me. We've been getting up together and out of the house in all weather—crunching through snow, under the umbrella in rain, walking in the early morning dark—since the first months after she was born. First carrying her in the Baby Björn, where she would nap sometimes for an hour, I walked Ruby around. Last year I walked the dog with Alice in a backpack, and now our daughter walks by herself, holding my hand, wanting desperately to be the one to handle Ruby's leash. We live on a busy street, so people often comment about how they've watched her grow up—neighbors or deliverymen who are out there early or see us at the same coffee shop or breakfast place.

"Ruby, stay here this morning," I said. "Don't worry, I'm not going to run every day. And you just sniff too much and get too crazy with the squirrels. I'm sorry, girl."

It was muggy hot, even at 6:30 this morning. Then a hard rain burst down. Only partly shielded by the stroller's visor, Alice was good about it. Both of us wet to the skin, we found a garage that was under construction. It was such an aggressively hard rain that it was fascinating for Alice to watch, the drops "going up" from the puddles. When the rain eased we jogged on to the coffee shop, where she got an egg and cheese on a bagel. It did feel good to run, if only a mile or so. And I'm actually not so stiff right now. We'll see in the morning.

Later in the day when I was coming out of work, I saw the blue Patriots El Camino driving past. I waved, but I don't think he saw me.

AUGUST 29 / 11:15 P.M.
MYSTIC, CONNECTICUT

When I watch football games on Sundays, I normally vacuum, fold laundry, piddle through other house chores, or do mindless tasks for work. This spring, though, we got rid of our television set. This is better because it's forced me to find a local place to watch the season among Patriots fans. Lisa likes it better, too, because I won't waste more hours watching every other game all weekend. We also live in a small house, so she and Alice won't have to walk in front of it or listen to the games in the background.

There are plenty of bars in my town, but none as far as I can tell that seem to have a true Patriots identity or a cadre of Pats fans. This is partly a Connecticut problem, because even though Mystic is on the Rhode Island border, we're still split geographically and culturally between Giants, Jets, and Patriots allegiances, just as in baseball any local around here may rightfully claim a connection to the Mets, Yankees, or Red Sox.

So I've settled on the Pier 27 Lounge, a bar owned by Angie's, the attached pizza restaurant. The Pier 27 Lounge is a short bike ride from our house on the other side of the river, and it has a banner that faces out toward the intersection that states "Mystic's Home of the NFL." The bar and pizza joint are in a boxy faded green building with a red roof—one of those places that has been around forever in your town and somehow survives year after year, but you've almost never been inside yourself and don't know anyone who chooses to eat there. This is especially true in our coastal village, which has several other bars and is famous for *another* pizza joint, regarding which the servers at Angie's are surely asked by tourists at least once or twice every summer day: "Is *this* Mystic Pizza?"

I went to the Pier 27 Lounge tonight and ordered a beer and a slice to watch the fourth and last game of preseason. The bar was sedate on a Thursday night: no rabid Pats fans, as I'd hoped. There was only one New England devotee, whom I'll call Chicken Little. He sat at a stool near the single window, which is blackened so you can't see in or out. Mr. Little is an older man with a paunch and a mousy gray mustache. "This is the year it's all going to catch up with us," he said to no one. "I'm telling you the Patriots are going to stink up the joint this season. This is the year the castle crumbles."

I sat by myself at a small table beside a wood vertical support post with a clear view of the largest screen. A bunch of people knew each other well. It's an older hangout sort of crowd. The jukebox was quiet, and it's too small and awkward a space for live music, dancing, or even any stand-up socializing. This is not a hook-up bar or a younger person's bar. At least by the presentation of football flags of every team hanging from the ceiling (knowledgeably arranged by division), a signed photograph of the New England Patriots cheerleaders on the wall behind the bar, and the manager's investment in a satellite plan to show every single NFL game—the only bar in town as far as I'm aware that does so—the Pier 27 Lounge does indeed strive to be Mystic's home for football.

Brady didn't play a single minute in tonight's game, but I still like to watch the rookies and others who are trying to make the roster. To tell you the truth, I can contentedly watch any meaningless football game. You give me the time, and I'll watch an entire, to the final minute, single-camera amateur local cable station showing a high school game involving a blowout of two weak teams to which I haven't the faintest connection. Besides, anytime the Patriots play the New York Giants now I can't help but watch, a veteran Patriots spectator with PTSBD (post-traumatic Super Bowl disorder).

This afternoon I was catching up on the summer's football news, procrastinating, because I still have been unable to frame my initial letter to Pressman James. This is now the last game of preseason.

Mr. Brady, are you ever lazy at all? Have you ever once gone in on a Wednesday and said something like: "Sorry, Coach Belichick, I just haven't been able to get to watching the film for our opener against the Bills. I promise I'll be ready tomorrow with all that stuff. Have you ever seen the movie North Dallas Forty? *Gisele and I just couldn't tear ourselves away from it last night. And then I fell asleep!"*

While I tried to make myself write another draft of the letter, I found a debate online spurred by an interview with a Pittsburgh Steelers defensive back named Ryan Clark who claimed that Tom Brady has been starting to "see ghosts." He meant that Brady is starting to get afraid on the field. He has been ducking, getting rid of the ball too fast and sloppily, cracking under pressure in the big games.

I've also been procrastinating with *Paper Lion*, the book by George Plimpton. In 1963 Plimpton participated in the Detroit Lions training camp as a backup to the backup quarterback in order to give readers an insider sense of just how far these guys are beyond an everyday Joe. At one point in the book, a star running back named Nick Pietrosante explains to Plimpton about how he's grown used to linebackers "clotheslining" him and how when he starts to worry about this he'll know it's time to retire.

Pietrosante says: "It's like when they speak of a quarterback *hearing footsteps.* When the quarterback thinks he hears someone coming up on his blind side, and he cringes, or throws hurriedly, his nerve's gone . . . that's usually the end of him."

I'm going to start watching for any cringing with Brady this season, to see if that Steelers defensive back has it right. Certainly though, the win/loss column bears out the reality that as he's gotten older Brady has indeed been "less clutch," or at least less lucky in the playoffs. Granted it's a team sport, but with him at the helm the team has been less able to win in the biggest games.

Again, Tom Brady won the Super Bowl his first season off the bench at age twenty-four, after a year as an understudy. He had come in to substitute in a game early in the season because the injured franchise quarterback Drew Bledsoe got hit so hard by a Jets linebacker that an artery tore near his ribs. Brady played so well over the next several games that Bledsoe, controversially, never got his job back. Brady continued to win, going undefeated in an unprecedented, unmatched streak, for his first ten games in the playoffs. He won three Super Bowls in four years. For perspective, the most any other quarterback has ever won in the NFL is four—and that would be only two other legends, Terry Bradshaw and Joe Montana, who did so over the course of their entire career. The only quarterback to win three rings, besides Brady, was Troy Aikman with the Dallas Cowboys.

Yet after winning those three titles, since 2005 Tom Brady has won seven and lost seven contests in the playoffs as of the start of this 2013 season. Brady has still won more total playoff games than any other quarterback ever and is now, with five, tied only with John Elway for the most Super Bowl starts. But Brady and his Patriots have lost their last two Super Bowl appearances, each in the final minutes. Both of these heartbreakers were to the New York Giants, steered by the quarterback I watched tonight, Eli Manning, who is Peyton's younger brother. When Manning came on the field tonight, Mr. Little said, "Damn you, Eli. You and your lucky throws make me ill."

In both these Super Bowls against the Giants, Brady had his team ahead with only a few minutes to go. Each time he sat on the bench and had to watch an extraordinary, once-in-a-lifetime catch that effectively won New York the championship. In other words, both losses came down to just a couple of plays that should've gone the Patriots' way, which would have rendered Brady with five rings and far and away the title as the undisputed most successful quarterback in the history of the game.

The first of these two Super Bowl losses to the New York Giants, in 2008, came down to an absurd catch by a second-string receiver named David Tyree from a desperate scrambling Eli. Tyree snagged the football with only one hand, trapping it onto his helmet, which extended the drive that would result in a touchdown a couple of plays later.

This catch snatched the Vince Lombardi Trophy from a perfect, undefeated Patriots team, spoiling what would have been the best season in history. The Miami Dolphins had an undefeated season over thirty-five years earlier, but their schedule had two fewer games and, more significantly, came before the era of free agency and the salary cap.

In February 2012, two seasons ago, the Patriots and Giants met again in the Super Bowl. Brady again had his team ahead in the fourth quarter—and driving in Giants territory. Brady hadn't been perfect, but he'd been under a lot of pressure all game from New York's monster defensive line. He still managed to set the record for the most consecutive completed passes in a Super Bowl. Now, Brady's one fault is that he can't really scramble. He's very slow. So he needs to be shifty in the pocket even as pass rushers swarm in. With 4:07 left in the game and New England up 17–15, Brady took the snap on second down with eleven yards to go. He dropped back and threw the ball to his left for about twenty yards through the air toward his trusted Wes Welker. It was to Welker's back shoulder, away from the approaching defender, and though Welker got both of his palms on the ball, he couldn't reel it in as he twisted up and backwards.

A completion here would have put the Patriots in field goal range, giving them another first down and likely the backbreaker. Thus, despite all of Welker's grit, endurance, skill, and stats as a Patriot for six years, he will unfortunately be best remembered for that drop of an imperfect but catchable throw from Brady to ice the Super Bowl. Instead Manning the Younger got the ball back deep in his own territory and subsequently chucked up a sideline bomb that a second-string receiver named Mario Manningham impossibly plucked out of the air over his shoulder, like Willie Mays. For Patriots fans this echoed the "Helmet Catch" from last time. The Giants finished the drive with a touchdown and the win and a furious Gisele slugging her springwater.

All of that is to explain why tonight watching Eli Manning march the Giants offense down the field, even if it was against our second-string defense, brought back bitter memories. Mr. Little sat on his stool and groaned and twitched.

Watching Brady standing on the sidelines this evening, I couldn't also help think about last season's AFC championship loss to the Ravens, just seven months ago. Brady and his offense could not score a point in the second half.

The analysts have been asking all summer and this preseason: "Is Tom Brady done?" Has his window to win another Super Bowl closed? Then, on the other hand, *Sports Illustrated* writer Peter King (who hasn't returned my e-mails yet) predicts that Brady will be the league MVP this coming season, that the Patriots will beat the Broncos in the AFC Championship, and that they'll then go on to beat the Seattle Seahawks to win the Super Bowl in February.

No matter what your prediction is for this season, though, there's no denying that Tom Brady is in the fourth quarter of his career. It's about this sort of debate that I want to ask him. But it's an insulting topic, and perhaps not one I should open with as we're having a catch:

Mr. Brady, how are you thinking about, preparing for, your eventual decline? Certainly you might have your best season this fall. You've still been having league-leading seasons the last few years, but eventually, and very soon, maybe even this year, you're going to have your weakest season and realize your best years as an athlete are behind you. You're going to know how to do something correctly, but your body, no matter how hard and expertly you've been training, isn't going to do it fast enough. Or you'll find yourself afraid in a way you never were before, making the wrong decisions—committing errors you didn't used to. How will you know when to quit?

This afternoon, before I biked over to the Pier 27 Lounge, a tow truck came to take the van to the mechanic again.

Ruby and I sat on our lawn and watched.

My neighbor Mike was walking by and said, "That doesn't look good."

"It's really not that bad," I said.

2

THE FOURTH-QUARTER COMEBACK

SEPTEMBER 2 / 9:45 P.M.
MYSTIC, CONNECTICUT

When I went to the pharmacy this afternoon to pick up my copy of *Patriots Football Weekly*, I saw that Tom Brady is on the cover of this month's issue of *Men's Health*. In the glossy cover photo he wears a black leather jacket with the collar flipped up. He's surrounded by teaser headlines in red: "The Pizza Diet," "The Vitamin That Boosts Testosterone," and "Will She Sleep with You? Find Out on p. 52." The headline across the quarterback's chest reads: "Strength + Focus / Win Like Tom Brady."

Also at the pharmacy I saw a slim brochure in the shampoo aisle with a photograph of Gisele, her golden locks streaming behind her bare bronze shoulders: "Healthier Hair with Every Wash."

SEPTEMBER 4 / 9:45 A.M.
NOANK, CONNECTICUT

Brady, the year you came back from your ACL injury, you told Sports Illustrated*: "Why would I even think of doing anything else? What would I do instead of run out in front of eighty thousand people and command fifty-two guys and be around guys I consider brothers and be one of the real gladiators? Why would I ever want to do anything else? It's so hard to think of anything that would match what I do: Fly to the moon? Jump out of planes? Bungee jump off cliffs? None of that shit matters to me. I want to play this game I love, be with my wife and son, and enjoy life."*

Before I go deep for a bomb and two yards off the line throw up my hand, pretending I'm wide receiver Randy

Moss, do you still feel that way? Can you tell me exactly where you got the courage to dream so big in the first place?

The students arrive tomorrow. I dread the semester. Not because I don't love the reading or because I don't like the students as people—it's that I can't bear to stand up in front of a class anymore. *Do you see what T. S. Eliot is doing here, blah, blah, blah . . .* And to grade the students' papers and judge them. I've also become the guy who goes home and complains about his younger colleagues, who he imagines don't work as hard or with the same respect as did he and his contemporaries. I wish I had the courage to quit outright and not care what people thought and pursue something else. Like with my backyard boat repair idea that I was telling Dumptruck about. I could paint, sand, and varnish all day long. A little carpentry, some fiberglassing. Ruby and I would work out there, listening to NPR and Patriots Radio. "Mystic Backyard Boats: Slow as Molasses, but Better Than New!"

Isn't it simply human nature, hardwired in our brains, to grumble and to want something else? I mean, I know I have only First World problems, and that I'm so personally and globally lucky with all that I have. But everything is by degrees, right? If I can complain, can feel so dissatisfied, while someone living in poverty in, say, Bridgeport, Connecticut, can look at me and say to his buddies, *He's got it made,* then why, by degrees, can't Tom Brady himself complain, while millions of men like me look at him and think *He's totally got it made*?

Brady, what do you complain about? Is it, er, people trying to meet you? Is it people in bars resting their own self-esteem on whether or not you complete a deep pass in the back of the end zone for a winning touchdown?

Which all brings me here, sitting in the van in the passenger seat after dropping off Alice at preschool. I'm avoiding work and looking out at the ocean with Ruby and thinking about the profound and unsettling bar-stool question I heard raised by two guys in their forties at the Pier 27 Lounge: "Would you change places with Tommy if allowed a full and complete switch, with no return and the future unknown?"

Brady, is there anyone with whom you would trade in that devil's deal? Will you give me a "to consider" short list?

SEPTEMBER 10 / 7:20 P.M.
MYSTIC, CONNECTICUT

I was catching up with a sea captain friend of mine, and he told me a story of how the quarterback once came aboard a ship he was working on in Boston Harbor.

"Dunkin' Donuts was doing a promotional event, and they had us string a huge banner between our two masts. Brady came on to give a sort of speech."

"About doughnuts?" I said.

"I don't remember. And I didn't talk to him personally or anything—it was open touring on board, and he walked around for five or ten minutes. I remember that he was definitely a big guy. You could tell he is a football player."

Captain Doug is six foot four.

"What would you ask him if you thought you could get a real answer?"

"What would he do with all that money?" the captain said. "How is he making the world a better place?"

SEPTEMBER 13 / 9:40 P.M.
MYSTIC, CONNECTICUT

I'm sitting in my office, scrolling through a long e-mail chain about trying to schedule a meeting that is going to be making a plan for a new time for weekly faculty meetings. I still haven't written to Pressman James or Brady.

The Patriots are 2–0. They opened to beat the Bills and then squeaked past the Jets. Both wins were ugly. Both were hugely important, though, since they were within the division, the AFC East. The easiest path to the playoffs, of course, is to win the division.

Tom Brady is clearly not in sync with the new receivers yet. With Gronk still on the injured list, Brady rarely threw to a tight end without it resulting in a drop or an interception. And the new wideouts dropped passes, tripped mid-pattern on their own feet, ran into each other, and jogged lazy routes. Against the Jets, twenty-two-year-old Aaron Dobson caught his first pass as a professional player for a wide-open walk-in touchdown, but then he dropped the next two passes. On another play, on third down with five yards to go in the red zone, within the other team's twenty-yard line, Dobson ran across the goal line and Brady clanked the receiver's ankle with the football. Incomplete.

"Brady's upset. And not knowing anything," the announcer said, "I'm going to blame Dobson." Was the play for Dobson to drop down at the line, away from the defender?

"When you're used to having a lot of guys that trust each other implicitly," the announcer continued as the Patriots settled for a field goal, "and then when you go out there with a bunch of rookies, man, it's frustrating."

They flashed to Dobson's face inside his helmet, his eyes wide and deer-like as he tried to gather what had just happened. Brady was upset, but it wasn't clear if the cause of his ire was his own throw or Dobson's route. The quarterback held his head as he looked up at the Jumbotron from the bench. He shouted "Wide open!" The next day, analysts on the sports networks and on radio debated as to whether or not Brady is patient enough with his rookie receivers. They argued about Brady's on-the-field demeanor. An odd contrast to his ever calm, even keel before the press or under center during a pressure point of a game.

Fifty years ago in *Paper Lion*, George Plimpton wrote about a tutorial he got from the Detroit Lions head coach about leadership on the gridiron. Coach Wilson used the Hall of Fame quarterback Bobby Layne as an example: "In his great years, when he was knocked over because someone missed a block, he'd shove a friendly elbow into the guy's ribs and tell him to forget it, that he could take it. The fellow'd think, *What a guy!* and the next time he'd do better—out of sheer respect for a quarterback who *could* take it. He'd block a bull elephant for Layne, or run through a brick wall for him. But then after a while it wasn't so easy to take, and Layne began to say, *You son of a bitch, you missed your block.* The players said Layne began to flinch. It wasn't that—he just lost his liking for it. So he chewed them out. That was all right if he was infallible, but no quarterback is, or ever could be, and his players began to lose respect for him—and when that was gone, his capability diminished at the same time. And when that really happens, you're done."

Bobby Layne retired at the age of thirty-six, which is Brady's age now. He had his birthday in August.

Tom Brady certainly was not infallible during these first two games. He missed at least one deep ball to an open man against the Bills, and in that same first game he fumbled the snap at the goal line, on fourth and inches in the third quarter. Brady hadn't lost a fumble in the previous twenty-seven games. But maybe it was the center's fault? And he's playing with all the new receivers, and no Gronk.

Yet two wins is two wins. And there are two reasons for optimism.

First, Brady led a fourth-quarter comeback drive with calm precision against the Bills to open the season in a hostile stadium. The Patriots were down by one point with 4:31 left in the game. Brady started his offense on his own thirty-four-yard line. It was a sunny day in Buffalo, a rabid sports town. The home crowd, which so craves a winner, was going ape with the opportunity to beat the Patriots on opening day. Brady led the team down the field to the Buffalo seventeen-yard line, setting up an easy field goal with a few seconds left in the game to chalk the victory. On this drive, Brady converted two clutch third-down passes as he threw seven straight completions. According to a football statistician named Scott Kacsmar, this drive was the twenty-seventh time in Brady's career that he led his team to a comeback in the final quarter.

The second reason, the added silver lining of these two ugly wins, is Brady's developing chemistry with Julian Edelman, who seems the only arrow Brady can pull from his quiver until the Return of Gronk. Especially because Danny Amendola is out for at least a couple of weeks with a sports-groin injury. Against the Jets, Edelman caught thirteen passes from Brady—a career high for the receiver. Edelman, I might add, is one of the few Jewish players in the NFL. Shalom, Mr. Edelman! Like Dumptruck, Edelman is fond of the karate chop when he makes a catch for a first down.

The first big connection between Brady and Edelman in the first quarter marked the first Patriots touchdown of the season.

Let me set the scene: It is third down with three yards to go, on the Bills' nine-yard line. The entire city of Buffalo seems packed behind that end zone under the direct sun, all wearing royal blue and carmine red and waving and slapping their thighs and pumping their poster-board signs and their huge letter *D*s and wahooing and bellowing to urge their defense to declare that this season will be different, that this season the Buffalo Bills will win the AFC East and go to the playoffs, that their men will overcome their history in which the New England Patriots under Tom Brady have beaten the Bills twenty of the last twenty-two times, and in which the Patriots and their quarterback and coach have won their last nine season-opening games, whether at home or away. The Buffalo crowd shouts and whistles and urges and hopes and fumes.

Tom Brady is in the shotgun with a running back behind him to the right. The quarterback seems to make everything quiet, to make time slow down. He might notice, however, one woman standing in her front-row seat, just to the left of the goalpost from his point of view. She's wearing a red Patriots jersey with the number twelve, and her hands are clasped in prayer with her fingertips urging beneath her lower lip.

Brady stands straight, relaxed, points to a linebacker, touches his fingers to his lips, and then dries them on the towel hanging from his waist. He leans forward with his hands out to receive the snap. He glances up at the play clock. Nine seconds. Eight seconds. Seven seconds.

Along with two other wide receivers, Edelman is lined up to Brady's left. Edelman is opening and closing his fingers in his red gloves when Brady abruptly shifts cadence and calls for the ball. Brady catches the low snap at his knees, dropping back inside as clean a pocket as a quarterback could ask for within a horde of three-hundred-pound men lurching with all their passion and force to put their helmet through his chest. While every single person on the field sprints and grapples furiously, and practically every fan in the stadium shouts and clenches his or her fist—except for that one woman still in prayer—Tom Brady stays relatively still: he stands perpendicular to the line of scrimmage, left shoulder forward, both hands holding the ball vertically at his chest. He stands with his feet slightly beyond shoulder width. He inches forward in the pocket.

Edelman has bolted off the line, seeking space between defenders as he angles in front of one man toward the center of the field and then to the right and into the end zone. Here Buffalo Bills safety Jim Leonhard begins to cover him, running in front and matching his speed.

Tom Brady pushes his tongue out of the right corner of his mouth, taps the ball twice with his gloved left hand, and steps into the throw with his left foot. He releases a spiral from almost behind his head—leaning forward like a baseball pitcher as he follows through in an open-fingered flow. A Buffalo defensive lineman reaches up and barely misses the ball, as does a Buffalo linebacker who jumps up and at his fullest fingertip extension also barely misses, more by a millisecond than by a millimeter. Brady's spiral has no wobble. Edelman must jump backward in full stride, to leap to face the quarterback and practically defend himself against the force of the football with his two gloved hands because the contact from the speed of the spiral and the awkward extension of his own body knocks him backwards, yet not so far that he cannot control his fall and still scrape his two cleats, left then right, into the grass, before the back line of the end zone. Touchdown!

Tens of thousands of heads sigh forward.

Only on replay do you realize that what appeared at first to be thrown inaccurately behind Edelman was actually the only place where this could have been caught. Brady aimed the ball at the back of the safety's helmet. The Bills defender had blanketed the Patriots receiver—anticipating that he was running for the back corner. Julian Edelman knew, perhaps by design, to be ready to collect the ball behind him, because the Bills safety was unable, despite flailing hands, to stop his own forward momentum as he fell to the turf, looking up to see the referee raising his arms to signal the touchdown. The touchdown!

Brady, did I get that right? Can you take me through that play? I'll pretend to be Edelman and I'm going to run the same route. (But maybe don't throw it so hard for me.)

SEPTEMBER 16 / 11:15 A.M.
MYSTIC, CONNECTICUT

Talked to my uncle Frank this morning, who is starting to get really excited about my mission to meet Tom Brady. I didn't tell him that I still haven't written to the press guy yet. My uncle Frank lives in New York City. He's a mystery writer in his seventies. He's big, heavy, toothless—a heavy drinker, former smoker, and he likes to say that he "dresses to confuse." Frank was once a superstar high school basketball player in Brooklyn. Literally one of the best in the entire city. I grew up with some framed newspaper clippings in my room. Uncle Frank got a scholarship to North Carolina, but then hated the whole scene so much he left after his first year.

Although he's a Jets fan, Uncle Frank finds Tom Brady "beautiful." He said he sees this as my spiritual pilgrimage up some mountain to meet a reclusive mahatma.

"But you can't just go meet Brady," Frank explained. "You need to have something to offer. Something secret. Some key to it all. You need to bring him some strategy or message or wisdom that's going to win Brady a fourth Super Bowl ring."

"Like what?"

"You're like Chingachgook in *Last of the Mohicans* or Queequeg or R2-D2 or some character like that. Maybe you've got a new play, or you've seen something in his technique that will change everything. You've got to *bring* Brady something. Something genius."

"Seriously?"

"Okay, I don't know yet. Let me think about it. I'll get back to you."

SEPTEMBER 17 / 9:45 P.M.
MYSTIC, CONNECTICUT

Went for a good run with Alice in the jogging stroller this morning. Lisa took her to preschool, while I spent the day avoiding work at home with Ruby. I called the mechanic again to find out about his progress with the van, but I couldn't get through.

I tried working on another draft of an opening e-mail to Pressman James. Do I write to James directly, or do I ask him to forward a note addressed to Brady?

Otherwise I scrolled through football websites, listened to sports talk radio, and generally grew anxious about Sunday's game against the Buccaneers. I wrote to the Denver Broncos pressman to see if I can get an interview with Wes Welker, perhaps even meet with him when he comes to town in November for his homecoming. I sent follow-up snail mail letters to sports journalists who haven't returned my e-mails. I wrote to contacts at the University of Michigan. I left a message to set up an appointment with a plastic surgeon in our area in order to find out if anyone ever came in to, say, hypothetically, get a little cleft folded in his chin.

Got here to the Pier 27 Lounge a bit later than I'd hoped. After this afternoon's Patriots-Buccaneers game I'm biking over to the elementary school for the first game of the season of our Middle-aged Football League.

When I arrived, I saw the blue Patriots El Camino parked in the lot! But I never saw the guy come into the bar to watch the game. Perhaps he was getting a pizza and watching it at home? I need to watch a Pats game with that super-fan.

It's much more crowded this afternoon compared with the last time I was here. I'm squeezed into a chair at the bar, because I couldn't get the spot by the vertical support that looks up at the biggest screen. With four different games playing on six televisions of various sizes, it's a bit hard to focus on the Patriots. When I arrived, the Bucs were already leading 3–0, but it seems like they should be up by more as they're sacking Brady, and their receiver is owning our top corner-back, Aqib Talib. Here's Talib:

The bartender wears a low-cut New York Jets jersey. One of the regulars joked with her about showing so much cleavage.

"I thought we were going swimming," she said, "so I brought my equipment."

I'm wearing my Patriots hat. A couple in their fifties at a corner table near the door wear their Patriots jerseys. The husband has number eighty-seven, Rob Gronkowski, and the wife wears number twelve. He's stoic. She's loud.

She screams things like "Jesus, get him!" A Washington Redskins fan, whom I'll call Dr. No-No, is far louder, though. He's a dentist during the week, but on Sundays he wears a Washington hat and jersey and is well known here by the regulars, who laugh as he grimaces and yells and his cheeks get sweaty and crimson. "No, no, no!" he froths this afternoon. "Why are you holding the ball like that? No, no, no, no, no! NO! What did you expect?!"

"Don't you love when he shouts at the screen?" says a grandmotherly woman. "As if they can hear him?"

On the most recent play, Brady failed to see two vastly open guys downfield for what would've been an easy touchdown.

"Dammit!" shouts Loud Brady Lady.

A family comes in to watch while waiting for their pizza. The mom holds an infant wearing a tiny number-twelve Patriots jersey.

"Hey, little Brady," says one guy.

"Can you stand it?" coos the grandmotherly woman to her friend.

At last, Brady connects with Kenbrell Thompkins for a touchdown—the rookie's first career TD—and the quarterback sprints over to give him a hug, as if trying to make up for the public criticism he's received for being too harsh on the new receivers. This is Brady's fifty-first game in a row with a touchdown pass—only three games away from setting the record. As the Buccaneers begin to implode, with their young quarterback throwing an untimely interception that is picked off by Talib, Brady makes them pay for it by ending the half with a clutch quarterback sneak and another quick drive to put more points on the board: 17–3 Patriots.

Oh, this is nice: they bring out free pizza and bar snacks during halftime. But I nearly got mobbed because I didn't anticipate it. The regulars positioned themselves for the delivery as soon as the half ended. They followed the trays as they came in, like a linebacker anticipating a throw across the middle. I was in the wrong place and in the way, annoying a couple of guys who had been looking at me funny from the start since I'm nursing a ginger ale and writing in a journal.

A woman in her late forties sitting to my right seems to know everybody. She's quick to laugh. We haven't talked at all, but we've shared a couple of smiles, and after I got a few scraps of the free halftime food after the initial rush, she got up and grabbed a couple of napkins and slid one beside my plate. Why don't I ever do kind things like that?

Opening the second half in bright, hazy Tampa Bay, the Patriots don't look clean on offense, but the Buccaneers look worse all around.

Brady just chucked an interception in the end zone, aiming for a rookie tight end. He tried to force it to the receiver between two guys. Maybe the rookie was supposed to come back aggressively to the ball, and it was a timing miscue?

"Brady is all washed up," whimpered Mr. Little. "The Patriots aren't even going to the playoffs this year. Stick a fork in us."

A tall bony-shouldered man wearing a Denver Broncos John Elway jersey that's too large for him, whom I'll call Gangly John, laughs at the interception and at Mr. Little's declaration. He launches into a diatribe to a couple of other guys about what a dumb pass that was. He punctuates the speech with "I fucking hate the Patriots."

The game's over now. The Patriots are 3–0.

Edelman is still the man, and the two rookie receivers did better this afternoon, but still plenty of drops. The defense has kept the Patriots from losing these first three games. They just flashed a statistic that the last time a New England football team started 3–0, they had an undefeated season and went on to the Super Bowl. The time before that, they *won* the Super Bowl after going 14–2. But, then again, they've started this season against three weak teams, including two rookie quarterbacks.

To the bathroom to put on shorts and go play some football myself.

9:30 P.M.

Back at home. A pretty good showing for our first MFL game this afternoon. We had enough guys to have three-on-three. Commissioner Lenny — skinny, balding, and always eager to make everyone laugh — welcomed everyone with his usual enthusiasm. We play at the elementary school in the outfield beyond a dirt baseball diamond. We mark the boundaries with sweatshirts. This is a good stretch of grass except there's a big manhole cover near one end zone, and the other end zone slopes down sharply into a fence. We play two-hand touch, two completions make a first down, five-Mississippi rush, one blitz every four downs, and no running plays or quarterback sneaks unless the defense rushes over the line of scrimmage. Kickoffs can be thrown, punted, or held between another's guy's finger and foot. We don't keep score.

I fancy myself the Wes Welker type on the field, with good hands and a bit quicker and shiftier than most of the other guys. But I'm going to try to take my turns at quarterback more seriously and really step back, stay relaxed, and zing clean spirals as the defender at the line speeds through his "one Mississippi, two Mississippi" (too quickly, of course) or barrels down on me for the blitz. Maybe I deftly step aside as the rusher falls past me with outstretched fingers, and I coolly scan to analyze the complex man-to-man defensive schemes of my MFL opponents before delivering the strike to Hoss and his sideburns in the end zone. Maybe I've diagrammed one of my well-researched plays, such as "Both of you go deep."

Lenny's vision for the league is that there should be as many all-out bombs thrown as possible, and that it's not so much how many connections there are through the air, but how aggressively receivers are willing to dive, to sacrifice our bodies for the pigskin. Lenny practices what he preaches and always ends the muddiest.

Brady, if you come and play with us someday, do you want to be steady QB? Or maybe for a change of pace you just want to play receiver and go out for bombs? Because among us, you'll be fast!

For this first game of the year, we six ballers represented a mix of professions: an urban planner, a child psychiatrist, an insurance sales manager, a research librarian, a middle-school science teacher, and me, a literature professor. We all wear running shoes. Lenny likes to wear jeans.

The elementary school is a good spot for our Sunday games because there's a good playground so our wives can hang out with their friends, too, as they watch the kids. At one point, a little one came sprinting down the hill and shouted "Daddy!" To which every single one of us turned. This was a good laugh. There are nine kids between us.

Injury report: I aggravated my back again when I tried

to avoid Kevin the librarian coming in for a blitz. About six months ago, I strained cartilage in my rib and sprained my back while I was ignominiously trying to secure a new car seat in the van. Paul the psychiatrist twisted his ankle badly, but shook it off.

Today was a great day. And tomorrow, no matter what I have to do, I'm mailing the letter to Pressman James.

SEPTEMBER 24 / 2:15 P.M.
MYSTIC, CONNECTICUT

Over the first three games, despite three wins, the New England offense is at the bottom of the league. Brady is himself in the NFL gutter for personal stats so far, a place he hasn't been since his first year in the league.

Other than Gangly John, someone who is especially enjoying this is Jerry Jackson, whom I heard back from yesterday. Jerry created and maintains the "I Hate Tom Brady" Facebook page.

Jerry started "I Hate Tom Brady" a few years ago and has a steadily increasing base of over ten thousand followers and commenters on his page, which is filled with invective about Tom Brady being feminine or gay, Tom Brady complaining about referees, Tom Brady needing to cry on Gisele's shoulder, and various other points of rage against anything associated with the New England Patriots. Occasionally, commenters declare that Tom Brady is the only player on which they wish career-ending injury.

Off his public web page, I found Jerry far more temperate and thoughtful than I expected.

"In general I just have never been a fan of Brady in the way he carries himself," he explained to me. "As in chasing refs down and screaming at them about calls. Looking for a flag basically any time he gets hit hard. I do think that he is a good QB, but perhaps one of the things that has always gotten to me the most was that he has almost always had an exceptional offensive line, and other than this year, he's usually had pretty good receivers. It seems that it is always Brady Almighty in the media, but his cast rarely gets any credit. I mean, if a QB like Matt Cassel can step in that system and win more than ten games, then you know they have a good system. All that, along with the Patriots organization. I'm not a fan of them and the kind of players they bring in."

He added: "And not to mention Spygate."

"Spygate" was a scandal early in the 2007 season in which the league discovered that the Patriots had been illegally filming defensive signals of the coaches of the New York Jets and other teams over the years. Belichick claims he thought he was working within the rules—that the practices, walkthroughs, and games that he filmed are not secret or closed in any way—anyone can watch everything with the naked eye, binoculars, whatever. (That's why when you watch a football game the coaches are always putting clipboards over their mouths when discussing anything about plays or strategy.) The league fined Belichick a half million dollars, which at the time was the highest fine in the history of the NFL. The Patriots got slapped for a quarter million dollars and the loss of their next first-round draft pick. The news show *60 Minutes* interviewed Belichick about the accusations, and U.S. senator Arlen Specter of Pennsylvania even inserted himself because of his disappointment in how the evidence was handled by the NFL. A man named Bryan O'Leary self-published an entire book on the subject of Spygate, dubiously claiming among other misdemeanors that Tom Brady has at times had an illegal extra radio frequency in his helmet during games. A few years ago a rumor circulated that the Indianapolis Colts had supposedly believed that when they played in Foxborough the Patriots bugged the visitor locker room.

For some football fans and analysts, Spygate and other intimations of cheating forever taint the accomplishments of the Belichick-Brady New England Patriots. Fans and journalists wonder why the NFL main office destroyed all the confiscated Patriots videotapes shortly after delivering the fine, an act that oozes some sort of cover-up that might go back to Belichick's earliest victories. "Haters" point out that the Patriots have not won a Super Bowl since Spygate.

Apologists of Spygate point out that every team tries to get an edge in all sorts of illegal ways and Spygate really wasn't that much of anything. It's just that the Patriots are more scrutinized since they win so much. I guess that's where I fall on the topic. Belichick seems monomaniacally and heartlessly committed to doing whatever it takes to win, but he does win, and there's not a fan outside New England who doesn't wish he coached for their team. After the Patriots were fined for Spygate in September 2007, they went on to have their undefeated season, steamrolling the league as they scored the most points in history. New England has posted a *better* winning percentage in the years *since* Spygate. Players and coaches also move around the league so much and cameras are everywhere these days, so any sort of egregiously illegal practices, some argue, could never be something so tightly held only in New England. Former Eagles coach Dick Vermeil once said about Spygate: "I know some things that have been done in the National Football League, and I could document them, if I wanted to, that are far worse than that ever came close to being."

Regardless, Spygate remains a regular point of punctuation for fans who dislike Brady, Belichick, and the Patriots. Five years on, it still comes up every season and in regular posts on the "I Hate Tom Brady" Facebook page. One commenter, for example, sent in a photo of an altered orange cereal box that says "Cheaties," with an illustration of Belichick holding a video camera.

Jerry Jackson often links to and creates his own "memes," which are altered photographs with funny taglines. Several memes on the page make reference to illegal filming. Others feature Brady on the field with a particular expression or pose, overlaid with a caption about the quarterback being unmanly or constipated. Jerry's most popular meme so far on his "I Hate Tom Brady" Facebook page was when he used a photograph of Peyton Manning in street clothes shaking hands with Tom Brady, in uniform, during warm-ups at a regular-season Patriots-Colts game. Before being traded to the Broncos, Manning had a season-ending injury with the Colts, who completely collapsed without their star on the field, mustering only one win for the entire season.

In the meme, Manning says to Brady: "Remember back in '08 when you got hurt and your team went 11–5?"

Brady says, "Yeah, so?"

"Just sayin."

I asked Jerry, a Broncos fan, what he would ask Tom Brady if given the opportunity.

"Perhaps I'd start with where he got his fashion sense from," he said. "I'm guessing his grandma. But in all seriousness, if I were expecting an honest answer, I'd ask him if he thought he could succeed on a different team with more average protection mostly. I think if he were on a team with your typical offensive line, he would put up more Jay Cutler-like numbers. Still good, but not what you get when you have time to read a book in the pocket."

Brady, do you ever go to the "I Hate Tom Brady" Facebook page? Can you resist? Can anyone ever get to the stage of confidence where he or she genuinely does not care what others think?

Instead of preparing for class and rereading Mark Twain's
Life on the Mississippi this morning, Ruby and I watched old
footage of Tom Brady leading the final drive of his first Super
Bowl win over a dozen years ago. They played the game in
the Superdome in New Orleans—Twain territory—so I figure there is a slight research connection.

This was the win that ended with The Photograph. The
Patriots played the St. Louis Rams, who had one of the best
offenses in league history at the time. Their veteran quarterback, Kurt Warner, had won the league's MVP that year and
put up staggering passing numbers. Las Vegas put the Rams
as favorites by an almost unprecedented two full touchdowns. During the regular season, the Rams had thumped
the Patriots in Foxborough.

Few thought the Patriots were for real that year. To advance in the playoffs, they had squeaked through a contro-
versial home game in a winter storm, thanks in part to an odd
"tuck rule," which reversed a play in the closing minutes in
which the Oakland Raiders sacked and forced a Tom Brady
fumble to end a drive toward their end zone. It's a play that
still enrages those on the "I Hate Tom Brady" page, not to
mention continually gnaws at the guts of Raiders fans. The
Patriots went on to beat the Steelers at Three Rivers Stadium
in order to advance to the Super Bowl to face the league's
best offense. The New England defense was solid and experienced, but their offense was green with a new quarterback.
Most thought it would be a blowout, but the Patriots led the
game until the fourth quarter. As Super Bowl XXXVI wore on,
the Rams powered back to tie the score, as most expected.
The Patriots defense was tired. St. Louis kicked off, and Brady
and the New England offense took over the ball on their own

seventeen-yard line with 1:21 left in the fourth quarter. No Super Bowl had ever gone to overtime before. The announcers began to discuss this as an inevitability. The Rams celebrated their comeback on the sideline.

Here's where Ruby and I shifted to the edge of the couch.

The famous coach-turned-announcer John Madden says: "And now with no timeouts, I think the Patriots with this field position, you have to just run the clock out, you have to play for overtime now. I don't think you want to force anything here. You don't want to do anything stupid."

Madden and every fan for both teams imagine an interception or a fumble or something that will give the Rams a chance for a field goal. Belichick surely fears the coin toss in overtime. So Brady lines up in the shotgun, calls for the ball — and almost gets sacked. He squeezes through the charging, grasping linemen to dump off a short pass up the middle.

Madden says: "Nah, I don't agree with what the Patriots are doing right here."

The camera cuts to Bill Belichick, calling the shots in his first Super Bowl as head coach.

Belichick directs Brady and his offensive coordinator to keep throwing. Brady completes another short pass, spikes it to stop the clock, and gathers his teammates into a huddle to call another play.

"This guy is really cool, though," Madden says. "I've been impressed watching Tom Brady on film and in television games and so on. But the way he's playing this game today. He's been very impressive with his calmness."

Another completion.

Madden: "Now I kind of like what the Patriots are doing."

When they cut to a close-up of Brady's young face, he looks relaxed. He could be on the field for warm-ups.

On the next play Brady throws the football out of bounds in response to a speedy Rams blitz from his blind side.

Now with twenty-nine seconds to go, the Rams linemen again rush Brady after the snap—but he steps forward in the pocket for what will be the most significant throw of his life so far, and perhaps still, as he guns the ball twenty yards downfield to receiver Troy Brown in stride over the middle. Brown continues running out of bounds to stop the clock.

"Amazing," says Madden. He admits he never would've had the guts to try this when he was a coach.

Brady has been perfect. The Patriots have it set up for a long but likely field goal to win the Super Bowl—the first for a franchise that has a long history of luckless performances and has never won the big game.

Brady hurries all his teammates up to the line in order to stop the clock with seven seconds left. When Brady spikes the ball, it bounces up in the air. He catches it above his head with his left hand, cradling the football aloft there for a moment in a gesture worthy of a Rafael painting.

Then, collegially, he flicks the ball to the referee and trots off the field as if this were halftime of an inter-squad scrimmage. According to author Charles Pierce, owner Robert Kraft watched this all from his executive box and "was stunned by the coolness of the gesture."

"What Tom Brady just did," John Madden says to some eighty million television viewers, "gives me goose bumps."

SEPTEMBER 27 / 10:30 P.M.
MYSTIC, CONNECTICUT

Van still not ready—waiting on a part, and it sounds like it's all going to cost over $1,500. I bought my ticket for the Broncos game, but my fund for this mission is depleting rapidly. I haven't heard back from Pressman James. In rereading my opening letter, I realize I probably dug myself a hole, because I begin by saying I want to talk to Brady about middle age, about being at the back end of his career. Who would want to talk about his own decline? I also asked for way too much. Here's part of what I wrote:

> Would the New England Patriots consider helping me to organize a meeting with Mr. Brady, perhaps even after the season is over? My absolute ideal situation would be (and I know I'm asking quite a bit here, but in the spirit of it can't hurt to ask):
>   - three one-hour interviews with Mr. Brady in February or March
>   - one press box / locker room pass for any upcoming game at Gillette this season
>   - one 30-min. interview with former offensive lineman Matt Light before the end of the season
>   - one 30-min. interview with rookie receiver Kenbrell Thompkins before the end of the season

- one 1-hr. interview with Jonathan Kraft before the end of the season
- one meeting with a person or group in the community that Mr. Brady has met with charitably

Too much, too much. In reading old interviews, even writers from magazines like *Esquire* just get a car ride with the man.

SEPTEMBER 29 / 8:15 P.M.
MYSTIC, CONNECTICUT

Halftime at the Pier 27 Lounge for the Patriots-Falcons Sunday night game. I got the little table I like by the support post. Loud Brady Lady and her husband aren't here, nor are many of the regulars. Gangly John is, though, with his oversize orange John Elway jersey. He's striding around among the Pittsburgh Steelers fans to gloat as his Broncos just rolled over another opponent this afternoon. Peyton Manning threw for four touchdowns, two to Wes Welker.

I might need to find another bar.

Good game of the MFL today, although when I threw the football on the first kickoff it bounced in the end zone and hurtled right over the fence. I climbed over and through the bushes, but as I came back with the ball, Hoss, ever the science teacher, gave me some advice: "Y'know that's poison ivy, right?"

Injury report: Paul the psychiatrist is out for the season with his ankle sprained. Hoss is complaining about his knees. "Can someone," he groans, "tell me *one* good thing about getting old?" My back has been stiff, but maybe more because I went for a harder run a couple of days ago—my first time without Alice and the jogging stroller.

Tonight would be a huge win for the Pats. I've been nervous all week. I've logged on to all the sports websites I know and read their predictions and analysis. The Falcons have a powerful offense and are tough to beat in the Georgia Dome.

The New England defense has been having a big game so far, led by their three stars on defense: team captain and nose tackle Vince Wilfork, team captain and middle linebacker Jerod Mayo, and their shutdown cornerback Aqib Talib. But Wilfork went down in the first quarter, so I'm curious to see if he'll be back in the game for the second half. The camera flashes over to Patriots coach Matt Patricia on the sideline, a heavy guy with a belt over his huge crimson shirt and a pencil sticking out of his black curly hair. He looks more like the pirate Blackbeard than a defensive coordinator.

I can see where the "I Hate Tom Brady" people get some of their fodder, because although the two QBs have played equivalent games through the first two quarters, the announcers fawned all over the Patriots' star quarterback at any opportunity but nitpicked any misstep by Falcons signal-caller Matt Ryan. Brady got his touchdown through the air, so now he's only two games away from the record.

Early in the second quarter a sultry young woman in her twenties, wearing a black tank top and jeans, had walked toward the door of the bar, presumably heading out for a smoke. She stopped to ask me what I'm doing.

"I, uh, I'm writing in my journal."

On her way back she leaned down and flashed me this huge smile: "I love your hat!"

It occurred to me, even if she's tipsy, that maybe she was kind of flirting with me? At one point after a big Patriots defensive stop, I heard her at the bar saying: "I'm so proud of them! They're playing so well. Fucking awesome!"

My loins ached.

But then washing my hands in the bathroom a few minutes ago, I caught myself in the mirror. I remember when I was young watching my dad looking at himself, really studying his face above the sink. It was not, I realize now, out of vanity. Because I just got hit myself with a long hard look at my own forty-three-year-old face and the graying, slightly wrinkling realization that the young woman at the bar was definitely not hitting on me. I'm old enough to be her father.

OCTOBER 3 / 9:35 A.M.
MYSTIC, CONNECTICUT

Thursday morning, just dropped Alice off at preschool and now I'm back in my office with the door closed. Three more days until the game against the Bengals. Until this morning I had been feeling good all week. Despite all the rookies and the new receivers and the injuries, the Patriots are 4–0. But it's a sixteen-game season.

Lisa has been away for work for several days. I really growled at Alice this morning when she was whining over and again about what sweater she should wear before we went out for a walk. I was cranky because it was taking us so long to get out the door, and my back was acting up, and the poison ivy itching, and I really needed a cup of coffee. I growled so loud at her that she covered her ears and began to cry. Ruby even walked back into the living room and began shaking. I feel awful about it. I talked to Alice later, before preschool, about how I need to work on having more patience.

Brady, does that ever happen to you? You've got three little kids. I see you there in the Georgia Dome on third and long backed up to your own end zone and the entire stadium and all the pressure on you, and you stay calm. Does that sense of calm, that way you handle stress, does it transfer to your life at home? Or do you have a temper with your kids like you have on the sidelines after a really poor play?

OCTOBER 5 / 10:30 P.M.
MYSTIC, CONNECTICUT

Reading Joyce's *Dubliners.* In 1914 James Joyce created a character named Little Chandler who wants to write poems, who has difficulty caring for his infant son. Little Chandler meets an old bachelor friend of his who has been traveling the world. He thinks: "Was it too late for him to try to live bravely like Gallaher?"

OCTOBER 6 / 9:15 P.M.
MYSTIC, CONNECTICUT

The Patriots lost this afternoon in the rain in Cincinnati. I listened to the game on the radio while Alice was napping, and then I listened to the rest as we played in the living room. The Bengals shut down the Patriots offense, allowing only two field goals. Tom Brady did not throw a single touchdown pass, the first time in more than three seasons' worth of games. In the loss, Brady and his offense were one of twelve on third down.

Despite the outcome, listening to the game on the radio was actually pretty enjoyable, since I know all the characters. I've been trying to explain to Lisa why I get so wrapped up in these games from week to week. Sports are like any television sitcom or drama or continuing series of novels or stories. It's no accident that both television and sports are clumped into "seasons." There are long-term characters, cameos, good guys, bad guys, and the built-in suspense each Sunday of who is going to score more points and win, eventually to hoist the trophy at the end of the season—to wear the golden ring. It's all there: glory, tragedy, violence, rivalry, revenge, racial tension, class tension, inspiration, myth, desire, deceit, and comedy. The announcers and cameramen sometimes even work romance into the story lines by flashing to various wives and girlfriends in the stands.

What's exceptional about sports compared with other TV shows and movies and radio plays is that the games are live. It's not scripted. Announcers and pundits and fans and players add drama off the field in advance and build narratives during the game, but the competition itself unfolds in real time.

As I listened on the radio, I liked imagining how my grandfather and father and Uncle Frank listened to the games, *imagining* their football. They rarely went to the Polo Grounds but with their ears to a box imagined their New York Giants —their personal Frank Giffords and Y. A. Tittles and Rosey Browns—in their minds' eyes.

To his press conference immediately after the loss in Cincinnati, Brady wore a high turtleneck sweater under a herringbone blazer and a plaid handkerchief in his breast pocket. With his bowl-cut hair still wet from the shower and buzzed high above his temples, he looked like some sort of well-dressed Scottish librarian or maybe one of those male models in fashion magazines who wear flood pants and a collared shirt buttoned to the neck in order to effect the nerdy look.

Brady, other than calling your grandma as Jerry Jackson would have it, where do you get your fashion sense? Gisele? Does UGG or another sponsor ask you to wear certain things? Do they lay out your clothes by contract? Do you have someone who checks on you just before you walk up to the podium after a game? Someone to make sure you're not hanging a boogie? Do you ever say to yourself —like with that thick white cardigan you wore at another press conference recently—"I can't believe I'm actually wearing this"?

At the press conference after the loss to the Bengals, Brady spoke graciously, if a bit more subdued than normal.

"It's a very good defense," Brady told the sportswriters. "I give them a lot of credit. Our execution needed to be really good, and it just wasn't."

Brady deflected any talk of his broken touchdown streak: "I'm just bummed that we lost." About the monsoon in the fourth quarter: "It's rain. It is what it is. You got to deal with whatever conditions are out there, and we just didn't do a very good job executing in them."

In recent days much of the discussion on talk radio and in the sports pages has raised the question of whether it might be time to start looking past Brady or at least trading him while he still "has value," while "he's still worth something." The league these days, they say, requires a more mobile quarterback.

I'm beginning to take these sorts of comments about Brady's decline personally, as if he needs my help. Give the guy a break, I think. It's a team game. One guy called in to one of the Patriots radio shows as if he were calling in to a counseling hotline. "When we lose I feel depressed all week," he said. "I just get so bummed out." I feel you, brother.

The Associated Press pointed out that if Brady ended the season right now, his completion percentage and passer rating for the year would be the lowest it has ever been, lower than at the end of his first season in the league. He's on pace to have his fewest touchdowns and most sacks since his second year as the starter. New England is currently second to last in the NFL for scoring percentage in the red zone. Talib and the defense, once again, bailed out the team in that Falcons game, and they held the Bengals to thirteen points, even without Wilfork—who is officially out for the season with a torn Achilles tendon. And now they are also without Tommy Kelly, the other veteran defensive tackle, who is injured for the year. The Patriots now field only rookies at defensive tackle.

Several people wrote in about the quarterback to *Patriots Football Weekly*.

"Do you think Brady is on the decline?" wrote a fan named Clarens Jarbeth. "And do you see Belichick making a move at QB in next year's draft?"

"I think I'm the biggest Brady fan," wrote in Guy Hilli. "However, don't you guys think he sucks from the beginning of the season? We can always use the excuses, injuries, rookie receivers etc., but he keeps missing open receivers, a lot of three and outs, very bad on third down. He is a superstar, he should pull the team to victories even on a bad day. He is not even close to what he used to be two or three years ago."

What is odd is that as I come to grips with Brady's decline, which seems like it's gaining steam downhill, I feel sorry for him. And for me.

OCTOBER 7 / 9:30 P.M.
MYSTIC, CONNECTICUT

"Alice, what would you ask Tom Brady?"

"What kind of toothbrush does he have?"

"Anything else?"

"No."

"Are you still excited to be Bill Belichick for Halloween?"

"No, Daddy, I really want to be a blue fairy now."

"Oh, no! Please? Daddy would so love if you were Bill Belichick, and, just like we planned, I'll be Tom Brady and Mommy will be Gisele."

"No, thanks, Daddy. I want to be a blue fairy now. And Mommy said she doesn't want to be Gisele. She never wanted to be Gisele."

"Please?"

"No, thank you, Daddy."

OCTOBER 8 / 10:15 P.M.
MYSTIC, CONNECTICUT

I hadn't heard back regarding my letter to Pressman James, so I wrote him an e-mail, to which he replied two minutes later! Here's exactly what he wrote:

> Sorry, I meant to respond last week. I had a chance to run this by Tom and he respectfully declined. Thank you for your interest. I hope I can help you in the future.
>
> Stacey James

This is bad news, but not unexpected. I do find it demoralizing, however, to receive an e-mail where the legal disclaimer is longer than the message.

In a rare moment of good judgment, I did not write back immediately. I need to think about my next move. I wonder if he did actually pass it by "Tom"?

OCTOBER 9 / 9:45 P.M.
MYSTIC, CONNECTICUT

Just watched the new *Frontline* documentary "League of Denial," about how brain researchers are beginning to learn how the multiple large and small concussions that players of football and other contact sports sustain can cause permanent brain damage, notably chronic traumatic encephalopathy (CTE). The documentary opens with the story of Mike Webster, who was the center for the Pittsburgh Steelers during all those years when they were the dynasty and when I was following them as a kid. Sometimes when Dumptruck and I played one-on-one football down at the park, I pretended to be "Mean Joe" Greene, and he pretended to be "Iron Mike" Webster.

Webster played in the trenches of the league for seventeen years. He was dead by the age of fifty with dementia, depression, slurred speech, and a variety of other health issues. Pathologists examined his brain tissue and diagnosed it with CTE, similar to that in the brain of boxers. Over the years more brain researchers have been involved, and though the National Football League's own doctors and researchers have repeatedly questioned these scientists' conclusions, the evidence as presented in this documentary is eye-opening, convincing, and scary. Certainly the creators of the show added dramatic flair in their cinematography and narration, mirroring the same deep voice gravitas of NFL *Films*, but the documentary was especially persuasive when it featured interviews with Hall of Famers, such as the former hard-hitting Giants linebacker Harry Carson, who had been concussed in games himself and now has a heartfelt, articulate concern for his and other players' health.

Researchers found CTE in the brain of an Ivy League college player who took his own life. The young man had never had a knockout concussion in a game—just the accumulation of hundreds of hits and jars to the head within his helmet over the years. Scientists then also found the disease in a high school football player who committed suicide months after receiving his fourth serious concussion playing football and other sports. The point is that CTE isn't isolated to men like Iron Mike who thumped in the trenches forever. Repeated hits to the head on the football field can cause severe and dangerous depression.

During Brady's midweek press conference, after the release of the documentary, a reporter asked the quarterback about the long-term impacts of concussions: "I'm just wondering how much of that is something you think about when you are on the field and also when you are off the field. Is that a topic you ponder or you just put it out of your mind?"

The camera is close up on Brady's face. He listens carefully, leaning in a bit. He pauses before replying with a smile that could be interpreted as smug, like there's an inside joke. But Brady's expression is hard to read.

"I don't think about it at all. Yeah, I'm not overly concerned."

He nods to confirm his position on the matter. Then he turns to another reporter to answer the next question about the New Orleans Saints' defensive schemes.

Really? Not at all? Is this something you don't want to comment on because the Patriots and the NFL advised you to stay out of it? Did you watch the documentary? Did Gisele? Your parents? Did your sisters watch it? The current president of the United States, Barack Obama, questions whether he would let his kids, if they were sons, play football. Tom, you have two sons. Do you have any doubts? Will you let them play? Do you think you might have CTE right now? I've heard you talk in one interview about how you do particular training, "building resiliency" to protect you from future head trauma. Seriously? Will you let doctors examine your brain after you die? Can you tell me the truth about what you think?

In my Literature of the Sea class, I'm teaching *The Log from the Sea of Cortez*, an adventure in the Gulf of California just before America entered World War II. At one point, authors John Steinbeck and Ed Ricketts discuss fighter pilots. They wonder if a pilot actually understood, actually thought carefully about what happened to his bombs after he dropped them, could he be effective at his job? Maybe I need to take Brady at his word, that he really does not think about it. Perhaps he will not allow himself to. Or maybe he calculates that it can't be more dangerous than driving around in an old Volkswagen van on a highway.

Then again, he is not twenty-four anymore, with that blissful ignorance, that blithe invincibility of that young gladiator eager for challenge and fame. I remember one hit he took early in his career when he did scramble out of the pocket and ran down the sidelines and a Buffalo Bills defenseman came at him with his shoulder and forearm, knocking Brady horizontal and sending his helmet flying off his head. The announcer, former quarterback Phil Simms, said at the moment: "That hit gave me chills. That was scary."

Brady has since learned to take care himself on the field, partly because he is too slow to put himself in harm's way, but also he rarely takes the risks of big hits. But he still gets sacked and thumped around every once in a while. So how could the documentary not affect him when it shows clips of other superstar quarterbacks, Terry Bradshaw, Steve Young, and Troy Aikman, all getting concussed severely on the field? All three of these Hall of Famers have expressed their concerns for others playing professional football, and Bradshaw speaks of his own depression and loss of memory. Yet all three have stayed involved in the sport as television analysts. Brett Favre, now forty-four, said in a recent radio interview that he's begun to start forgetting things.

The documentary "League of Denial" ends with the suicide of Junior Seau, a star linebacker with whom Tom Brady played on the Patriots. Seau killed himself at the age of forty-three. Which is my age. Some say Seau shot himself in the chest so that his brain could be examined. Researchers did find CTE in his brain.

Surely in part to counteract the bad press about concussions and accusations of its disregard for players' safety, the National Football League has donated millions for further research and the analysis of brains and tried to firm up concussion protocols on the field. The league has begun a "heads-up campaign" about teaching kids to tackle properly. The league has also begun a "Together We Make Football" promotion, inviting fans to send in a video or a piece of writing about why football has been significant to their lives. The winners will get tickets to the Super Bowl and a role in the NFL's own feel-good documentary.

I'm thinking about when the Patriots played the Atlanta Falcons two weeks ago, when young Aaron Dobson dove across the middle of the end zone for a catch. His head bent violently up then backward when a defensive back flew in from the other direction to knock down Brady's pass. Tom Brady sprinted into the end zone—not to Dobson on the ground, but toward the referee, looking for unnecessary roughness or a holding call to sustain the current drive for six points.

OCTOBER 12 / 8:45 P.M.
MYSTIC, CONNECTICUT

Out for dinner on our wedding anniversary tonight. I thanked Lisa for being so good to me, for letting me do all this stuff to try to meet Brady.

"You know I'd rather have you than Tom Brady," she said.

"I love when you lie to me," I said as we clinked glasses.

OCTOBER 13 / 3:15 P.M.
MYSTIC, CONNECTICUT

"It looks like it'll just be the five of us today."

"I'll play steady QB, because my knees are still bothering me."

"Can you go out every once in a while? Play steady offense?"

"Because *you* want to play QB?"

"What's wrong with that?"

"Is this part of your stalking campaign?"

"Because I want to play QB sometimes?"

"Because when you play QB you're concentrating too hard!"

"Lenny?"

"Hoss is telling the truth. This season you *have* had a too serious look on your face whenever you're QB."

"I'm working on my seven-step drop."

"How about working on throwing it near my hands?"

"Brady says when you throw a spiral you need to cup your hands like a C, not a U."

"How is the stalking going, anyway?"

"I prefer to think of it as more of a journalistic meditation on Tom Brady. I'm preparing for a serious interview. I'm like Barbara Walters or Terry Gross. Or Morley Safer."

"Like Oprah?"

"You're stalking him."

"Admit you're sexually attracted to Tommy Terrific."

"I am not a stalker, okay? I'm not showing up at his house or waiting outside the locker room or anything like that. I'm not sending him packages with pasted cutout letters from magazines. This is a serious literary endeavor."

"You're a stalker claiming that watching football is investigative journalism."

"Is anyone paying you to stalk him?"

"Can we start playing, please?"

"Only if I get to be steady QB. My knees really hurt. One thing! Can someone tell me just one good thing about getting older? Just one good thing."

"Do you guys think I'm going to meet him ever?"

"Nope."

"Never."

"Not a chance in hell."

"Hell, yeah, you will! I believe! Just bring him here so he can throw us bombs, and I can dive into that pile of leaves."

"Anyone want to watch the game with me tonight at Pier 27?"

"I've got stuff to do for work tomorrow."

"C'mon! This is a huge one tonight against the Saints."

"You can come over my house if you want. I got the kids because the wife's got her night out with the ladies."

"Can someone please kick off the fargin' ball?!"

11:45 P.M.

I'm finally sitting back down at the table, and I still can't believe it.

Unbelievable! Un! Buh! Lievable!

I was giving high-fives to strangers. I hugged Loud Brady Lady's husband. We were all dancing. Gangly John had to walk out. This is Brady's second fourth-quarter comeback of the year. It's got to be one of the craziest of his whole life.

It went down like this: the Patriots dominated the first half, but then the Saints came back, in part because Aqib Talib got injured—he had eliminated their top Gronk-like tight end, Jimmy Graham. In last year's AFC Championship game, Talib got injured before the half, and the Ravens came back to stomp all over the Patriots. So tonight, in the fourth quarter, with less than three minutes to go in the game, New Orleans was up by a single point. Brady couldn't get a drive going because of drops from his receivers.

"This is all going to get fixed when Gronk comes back," said someone at the bar.

"Season's over," whimpered Mr. Little.

Belichick chose to go for it on fourth and six inside their own thirty-yard line!

Gangly John shouted: "Miss it! Choke, Brady, choke! Belichick you hooded douche bag!"

Brady found Dobson — who couldn't hold on.

"Aaron *Drop*son," sighed the guy I call Nick Name, because he's got one for every player.

"Dammit!" shouted Loud Brady Lady.

But the Pats defense stopped Drew Brees and the Saints yet again. New Orleans kicked a field goal. Saints 27, Patriots 23.

On their next possession Brady got it back, and we were all ready for a signature Tom Brady fourth-quarter touchdown drive. Two-minute drill. Brady promptly threw a deep bomb toward Julian Edelman far to the right and too short. Intercepted.

"Yes! Nice one!" Gangly John cheered.

"I called it," Mr. Little said.

I confess. I lost the faith. That moment, that drive, was supposed to be what made Tom Brady the greatest. Loud Brady Lady's husband in his Wilfork jersey sensed the collective despair. He said: "Good thoughts, everyone. Good thoughts."

The announcers discussed how this is a tough loss for the Patriots at home and how now the Saints are still undefeated. Half the crowd at Foxborough on a Monday night left their seats to beat the traffic.

Yet even without Talib, the New England defense once again held the Saints, who, as Belichick used his time-outs, could not run out the clock. The Patriots got the ball back one last time with one minute to go, no time-outs, and needing a touchdown from seventy yards away.

Gangly John began pacing, even though the Broncos had finished crushing the Jacksonville Jaguars already today. Wes Welker got his eighth TD of the year, leading the league so far, and Manning the Elder set an NFL record for the most TDs at this point of the season.

Loud Brady Lady shouted exhortations. For the first time this season Pier 27 was packed primarily with Patriots fans. The bar was standing room only. A couple of people put their beers on my table. Brady zinged a long dart to Julian Edelman, who took a huge thump in midair—but held on to it.

"Go, Julian!" screeched Loud Brady Lady.

Edelman had been unreal today, including his punt returns. Then Brady connected with journeyman Austin Collie. And then a quick hurry-up to Dobson, who was able to struggle out of bounds to stop the clock. Everyone in the bar was standing now. Brady tried to find Edelman twice near the goal line but couldn't quite connect. The receiver looked tired. Brady then converted a fourth-and-four toss to Collie, who got tackled before he could get out of bounds. Brady ran up and spiked the ball. Ten seconds left at the Saints' seventeen-yard line. Brady dropped back and found deep in the corner of the end zone rookie Kenbrell Thompkins, who leaped backwards and nabbed the spiral at full extension with both hands. He dropped back to earth, inbounds, in stride. Touchdown! Touchdown! Touchdown! Touchdown!

I was shouting! Hugging strangers! Everyone shouting! Touchdown! Touchdown!

"Is there a flag?!"

"No flags!"

"Touchdown! Touchdown!"

"Unbelievable!"

"It's never over until it's over!"

"Unbelievable!"

"The Comeback Kid!" shouted Nick Name.

A man in his late twenties yelled: "Oh my god, right now I would put my lips around Tom Brady's—!"

"Unbelievable!"

"The Saint of Foxborough!" shouted Nick Name.

"I hate every single one of you!" Gangly John hissed.

The television announcer: "One of the most unbelievable finishes from one of the most unbelievable quarterbacks in the history of the NFL!"

"We did it, honey!" said Loud Brady Lady's husband.

Some guy I didn't know ran over and gave me a high five. "Unbelievable!"

The camera cut to the disgusted Saints defensive coordinator Rob Ryan. The Patriots quarterback, *our* quarterback, jogged off the field.

As I scribble this all now, the Pier 27 Lounge has still barely cleared out. Everyone is too happy! Back on the Tom Brady bandwagon! I know I'm going to go home and watch that play thirty times, because I have too much adrenaline, I'm not going to fall asleep until 3 a.m., and I'm teaching first thing in the morning. Touchdown! Touchdown! Touchdown!

What a win! Unbelievable! Un! Buh! Lievable!

OCTOBER 14 / 9:50 P.M.
MYSTIC, CONNECTICUT

Man, it felt great to be on the right side of that win last night. I heard a stat this morning that Brady has the highest winning percentage at his home stadium among all quarterbacks since at least 1950 — when they started to collect this type of information.

I have to say, though, that as I was watching the game I couldn't help thinking about the hits. During one play in the second quarter, I cringed when a woman sitting at the bar yelled: "Hurt him!"

In the first half, offensive lineman Dan Connolly was knocked out with a concussion. "Next man up" is the proud Patriots mantra whenever someone gets injured.

I worry most about the slot receivers — the quick, little tough guys, the Wes Welker and Julian Edelman types, who are always catching passes over the middle of the field. Danny Amendola, in his second game back after his sports-groin injury, took a vicious hit as he sprinted toward the sideline on a reverse. The defender dove in, colliding his helmet into Amendola's. The receiver was knocked cold so instantaneously that he did not put his hands forward to break his fall. Amendola landed on his chest and shoulders, head down, with his arms limp and backwards. Face in the turf, he was unconscious until they picked him up. A guy at the bar shouted: "Oh no, get up, Amendola. You can't be hurt again." The receiver looked hobbled and dazed. The medical staff escorted him into the locker room, surely uninterested in the cameras watching an examination on the field or zooming in on the player's glassy expression.

Replacing Amendola was another slot receiver named Austin Collie, a guy who has been off the field for nearly a year because of three major concussions and then a knee injury. The Patriots picked him up during training camp, and he's been on and off the New England team from week to week, based on Belichick's needs for Sunday.

"Not Concussion Collie," said Nick Name, as the receiver jogged onto the field to replace the downed player.

Despite the high from the win against the Saints, I'm wondering what I'm supporting here with the concussions and violence on the field, what it brings out in the fans, and even all the off-the-field criminal activity—like the Hernandez murder charge. I mean, what exactly am I supporting with my time and money?

OCTOBER 29 / 10:20 P.M.
MYSTIC, CONNECTICUT

How long has it been since Ruby died? I don't even know. Two weeks. I haven't been up for writing since it happened.

Lisa called at work to say Ruby had gotten out of the yard again, and Alice needed her attention. So I biked home. I took my time leaving work because Ruby is always getting out and scampering around the woods behind our house, sprinting after squirrels and the pair of neighborhood feral cats. I kept thinking I had found the spot in the fence. I'd patch it, but then she would get out again several weeks later. (I'm thinking now there's one tree she must've kicked off of to climb *over* the fence?) When I biked down the hill and saw some strange car pulled over on the other side of the road and one in our driveway—I just knew. The women had stopped and helped put Ruby in the back of our van on a sheet for the blood. Lisa had Alice in the car seat and had planned to go to the vet, but found herself too shaken up to pull out of the driveway. She saw it all, heard the screech of tires, now has the whole impact horribly branded in her memory. Alice didn't see anything—she was on the back porch scooping out a pumpkin. Ruby had been killed on impact. I put my head to the dog's chest, my fingers to her eyelids, and I knew she was dead. But I drove to the vet at ninety miles per hour anyway, sobbing, just for them to tell me for sure she was gone. If I had only given her more exercise, or hired somebody to build a six-foot fence instead of patching it, or even if I biked home ten minutes earlier. She was by far the best dog I've ever had or even ever met. I thought she'd grow old with us. My fault.

NOVEMBER 1 / 11:30 A.M.
MYSTIC, CONNECTICUT

A couple of weeks ago I sent Pressman James my previous books in a big envelope, on the back of which I drew a huge color cartoon of Pat Patriot leaning down and writing in a book. I'm hoping Pressman James has a sense of humor, and that he'll reconsider speaking with Brady about a visit. Still no response, though.

I saw online that at the New England Patriots Halloween party, Tom went as the Cowardly Lion from *The Wizard of Oz*. The paparazzi photographed Gisele as a supermodel version of Dorothy, with a super-short gingham housemaid dress and red spiked heels, swinging a little basket with a stuffed Toto.

In the end Alice decided she *did* want to be Bill Belichick. This snowballed as she got huge laughs from anyone she  told about it. Alice is a really smart kid, thanks to her mother's genes. She is also endlessly social and chatty—from where she gets this we have no idea —so her being Belichick is that much more ridiculous. She certainly likes to be in charge, so that fits. Thanks to a secondhand kids' clothing store, I was able to fit her out with a tiny gray cutoff sweatshirt with a Patriots jersey over the top. She wore headphones. I tied a "play sheet" to her sweatshirt that showed a couple of *X*s and *O*s leading toward a huge candy corn. I put a red sock challenge flag in her pocket. I was proud of myself, and she found it hysterical, too—maybe because it cracked up everybody at our friend's Halloween party.

For my costume I carried around a football and wore a TB number-twelve youth medium jersey I bought at a sporting-goods store. It's pretty snug—they didn't have a kids' large in stock—but it did the job, as did the on-sale price. Lisa dressed as a referee.

Now Alice goes up to everyone, stranger or friend, and asks: "Want to see my Bill Belichick face?"

At the house, everyone in bed. On the couch. Without Ruby.

I'm starting to develop a sense of the Pier 27 Lounge ecosystem. Under the heavy wood beams and between the warm pink stucco walls, the watery stained-glass light, I feel sometimes on game day as if I'm in an autumn corner of a forest, with a collection of other amphibians and insects clambering around an overturned log.

Opposite the bar from Mr. Chicken Little are the Pittsburgh Steelers fans. They are the loudest and proudest at Pier 27. They have their own Steelers Alley, and the bar's management has let them hang a photograph of the Pittsburgh locker room and pin up the team's signature yellow "terrible towels" on the wall and on the supports around their section. Whenever the Steelers have a big play they shout, "Downtown, baby, downtown." When the Steelers score, these fans order a shot and toast to the team and the owners: "To the Pittsburgh Steelers and the Rooney Family! God bless them all!" They gulp their shot and slam the glass in unison on the bar.

From my favorite table, I watched over the last two Sundays the Patriots split between two AFC East division foes. They lost to the Jets away, but beat the Dolphins at home. Both games were ugly.

Against the Jets, Brady and his offense stunk, even with —finally, at last—Rob Gronkowski back on the field. Brady fumbled twice, both recovered by the Patriots, and he threw an interception that the Jets returned for a touchdown when he tried to force one to Gronk. In the fourth quarter, thanks to their defense, the Patriots were still in it.

"I don't care if he's been one and ten for third down," the announcer said. "He's still Tom Brady in the late stage of the ball game."

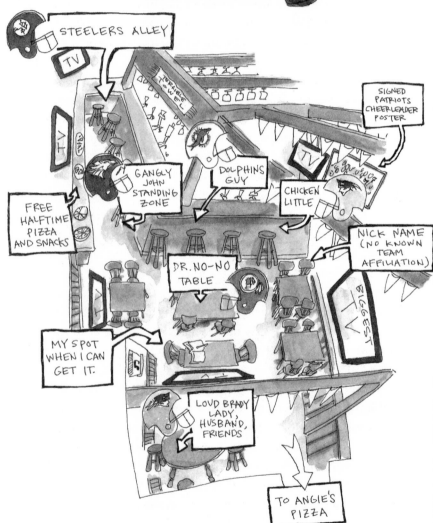

Brady got the ball back at his own eight with just over two minutes to go.

"Tom Brady, master of the comeback," the other announcer said.

I nervously sipped my ginger ale (I had an MFL game afterward).

And Tom Brady was at first, partly, his former young, clutch self. Even with a swollen throwing hand he had injured during a first-half sack, the QB drove the team into field-goal range to tie the game.

The Patriots won the coin toss for overtime, but Brady couldn't muster any more magic after Aaron Dobson dropped another pass. Without their best players at all three levels of the defense—Wilfork and Mayo out for the season and Talib injured for a few weeks—the Patriots couldn't hold off New York, even though the Jets have an error-prone rookie quarterback. The Patriots lost by a field goal.

Then last Sunday against Miami the vibe was a little tense at the Pier 27 Lounge, because the regular whom I call Dolphins Guy, with his high forehead and his corner seat at the hub of the bar, is a devoted fan of his Miami team. He's a friendly, soft-spoken man. Even I knew it would be impolitic to cheer too loudly. Nick Name shouted, "Squish the Fish!" once, and then called their quarterback Ryan "Tan-his-hide." Upon which everyone turned and looked at Nick with hairy eyeballs.

On Brady's first play of the game against the Dolphins he threw an interception. He tried to force it to Gronk again. I blinked, and they were down 17–3 at the half. At home, at Gillette Stadium. The cameras regularly focused on Brady's swollen throwing hand, which he at any free moment tucked in the pocket sleeve hanging from his belt. The Patriots eked out a win in the end, but it was more on Miami's errors, a few helpful calls from the referees, and solid Patriots defensive work, sacking the Dolphins' young quarterback five times in the second half.

It's amazing the Patriots are still leading the AFC East and have such a good overall record at 6-2. Unless they collapse, they should earn a playoff spot. The Denver Broncos, the real powerhouse in the AFC and surely the conference gatekeepers to the Super Bowl, are a far more convincing 7-1. Peyton Manning and his offense continue to roll over teams. At Pier 27 last Sunday they played the Redskins. Dr. No-No wore his Washington helmet as he groaned at his table: "No, no, no, no! Do not let him get behind you! NO! What kind of tackle is that? Oh, no!" He watched Manning throw four touchdown passes.

NOVEMBER 2 / 8:30 A.M.
MYSTIC, CONNECTICUT

Dear Stacey:
Congratulations on Sunday's win against the Dolphins! In the hopes that I'm erring more toward persistence rather than annoyance, I'm writing to find out about the possibility of any of the below, such as an interview with one of the rookie receivers or Julian Edelman? I sent a package of two books to your office in the hopes of demonstrating the type of work that I do.
Gratefully,
Rich

9:45 P.M.
Seeing how I've been getting nothing back from Pressman James or practically anyone else, I decided I need to return to The People to gain some wisdom. Lenny's wife Elke is in

many ways a bigger Patriots fan than he is. She let me interview her as she waited on the corner to pick up their girls at the bus stop.

Growing up, Elke never followed professional sports of any kind. She met Lenny in her twenties. When they watched a Super Bowl together in a bar, he started explaining the rules to her, and she began to have fun.

"Before then all I would see were a bunch of large men in lots of pads standing around. You would just see the same plays over and over again. I never bothered to try to understand it. Until," she laughed, "I saw Tom Brady.

"It was Brady's first season that I started really watching. The year he came in for Drew Bledsoe. I just love the story of Tom Brady. The backup quarterback. The guy that everyone passed over. I just love those underdog stories. And he was so clean-cut. The Patriots seemed so respectable. They were okay to root for."

"But what is it exactly," I asked, "that makes him so attractive?"

"He's certainly very attractive physically." But she went on to explain that when she first got into football, she listened to Brady's weekly radio interview during her Monday morning commute. She was impressed with his humility and demeanor, whether after a win or a loss. How he spoke so well of the other team and his own teammates.

"So that's very attractive, how he talks. And I also appreciate his poise under pressure. As an athlete and as a person, he can handle these very intense situations and still come out on top."

"But is there something *in particular* that makes him so physically attractive? Like his cleft chin?"

"It's the whole package. I never pick out something like that. Did you know that he and I locked eyes once? Lenny and I took the girls to training camp, and Brady was right there on the other side of the fence. I'm sure he and I looked at each other. Later, though, I realized I was carrying one of the girls on my shoulders, who I think was about the same age as one of *his* boys at the time, and also blond. So he was probably looking at her. But in my fantasy, he was checking me out."

As we sat waiting for the bus, Elke told me she didn't have any questions for Brady specifically. She simply wanted to get past the drooling stage. "I'd like to just shoot the shit with him. Sit on the couch. Have him listen to me!"

We joked that she'd say things like: "Can you believe Gisele said that?" or "What's on your to-do list today, Tom? Going to the hardware store to buy a new rake?"

Elke told me that as the years have gone by, Brady and the Patriots have lost their luster: "There was that thing with Tom Brady and his personal life, and that took him down a couple notches. When he had his girlfriend Bridget Moynahan, and he dumped her when she got pregnant, and then starting dating Gisele Bündchen, and then *she* got pregnant. Right? I don't think that was the most stand-up thing to do." She laughed. "But I don't know all the details."

"I don't either," I said. "I heard that maybe he didn't know Bridget Moynahan was pregnant when they split up. And it was a little while until he had a kid with Gisele, after they got married."

"Right, he might not have known with Bridget. And I'm willing to give him the benefit of the doubt! But then there was Spygate. And all this stuff about concussions. The big corporation of the NFL, Welker leaving. It just seems it's all a big business. I'm still a Patriots fan, I still love Tom Brady, but it's not the same now that I'm older. Although I do still say *Hi, Brady* anytime I see him on the TV."

"Do you think he's going to get caught up in some scandal someday?"

"Has any big celebrity ever escaped?"

"You think it'll be a Bill Clinton kind of thing?"

"I don't want to think about it, if you want to know the truth. I just hope not."

"Do you think I'm actually going to meet him?"

"Yes, yes. Totally. I think it is going to happen. If you really want this! To have that moment. Like winning the big game!"

"How do you think I'll respond?"

"Well, that's the real question," Elke said. "Because if it were me, I would be the adoring fan and stumble all over my words and make a fool of myself, but that's not what I want. I want to just shoot the shit with him. I want us to be buddies. To have some mutual respect. To have a normal conversation. But that's never going to happen."

"Sometimes it's hard to talk to really tall people," I said.

"I know! I was just at a party this weekend with a lot of tall people, and it made me kind of uncomfortable."

"What if he's really a prick?"

"I can't let myself believe that," Elke said. "No, he can't be. He's not that good an actor. Oh, look, it's here!"

"I bet Tom Brady doesn't wait for the bus."

"I bet he wishes he could!"

NOVEMBER 3 / 12:50 P.M.
EN ROUTE TO BOSTON

I was lucky to make this train. Even after all the time at the mechanic, now the van's engine won't turn over. A whirring sound from somewhere underneath the alternator kept spinning even when I took the key out of the ignition. I tried to start the van a few more times, but no luck—and the whirring continued. With no time to figure this out, I rushed to get my bike. I told Lisa I had to go, but I assumed that the whirring sound would have to stop when the battery ran out? She gave me a disapproving look. I tried the ignition one more time. The van started up on a final Hail Mary. Yes! I chucked the bike inside for backup, drove to the station, chose a parking space that provided easiest access for a tow truck, and then, hearing the train's horn in the distance, leaped across the tracks. The whirring stopped as I made it to the opposite platform.

11:45 P.M. / EN ROUTE BACK
TO MYSTIC, CONNECTICUT

I watched the Patriots-Steelers game tonight at the Fours, which is supposedly the largest sports bar in Boston and was rated by *Sports Illustrated* as the best sports bar in the country. I wanted a true Patriots fan experience among the faithful and undivided—and this seemed an especially good time to not be at Pier 27, with the Steelers having such a bad season so far and Steelers Alley sure to be ornery.

It turned out it *really* was good I wasn't in Mystic, because the Patriots pulled away from the Steelers in the second half with their best offensive game of the season. It became a rout. Everyone was healthy on the offensive side of the ball. Gronk caught nine passes for 143 yards and a TD, Dobson caught two touchdown passes, and even Amendola caught one in the end zone. This was by far Brady's best game of the year and statistically one of the best of his entire career. No fumbles, no interceptions, 432 yards passing.

This is all on the heels of more serious suggestions on blogs and talk radio that Belichick should consider trading Brady, even after his epic last-second comeback drive against the Saints. The memory of so many fans is one game, particularly the younger ones, and the media needs a story every day. I've been thinking: lay off the guy. So it's been his worst season ever. So far. They're winning, right? And tonight confirmed the quarterback's not going anywhere soon.

Particularly sweet tonight was Brady's eighty-one-yard

bomb to Aaron Dobson, who, like Randy Moss used to do, threw his arm straight up to signal that he was about to absolutely fly past Steelers safety Ryan Clark—the same Ryan Clark who this past summer spoke about Tom Brady starting to see ghosts.

Maybe I'm exhausted from all this running around, from missing Ruby, and because I was up with Alice at 4:30 this morning, but other than Brady and the Patriots' performance against the Steelers, I'm not feeling that excited about the victory as I ride the train home. The scene at the Fours was nothing like I'd hoped, despite being across the street from the Boston Garden, where the Celtics and Bruins play. It had a massive horseshoe bar that's larger than the entirety of Pier 27. Every inch of wall space was packed with memorabilia representing all Boston sports teams. There was a huge framed Brady jersey at the head of the bar, and the beer and my burger were excellent, too. But even with all that, I felt no warm camaraderie here for a fellow Patriots fan making the trip up from Connecticut. I think for some ridiculous reason I imagined it would be like walking into Cheers, and some guys would invite me to a big table of Pats fans and we'd all shout together. It was nothing like that. At first I sat right next to a young guy wearing a Brady jersey, which was promising, but he was all about fantasy football, clicking on his phone beside his friend who was wearing an Arizona Cardinals jersey and also tapping away. They watched three games at once.

The kid in the Brady jersey and his friend left before the Patriots game started, along with a huge shift of other people coming and going between the 1:00 and 4:30 games. So I sat at the bar next to a Minnesota Vikings fan who brooded, still stunned by a heartbreak loss of his team to the Dallas Cowboys. The crowded bar was sedate and quiet. Nearly everyone spread around and stared at the more than forty television sets. A chirpy clump of twenty-somethings wore Patriots gear and stood near my stretch of the bar, but they hardly watched the game. There were actually too many TVs at the Fours. Too many nooks and too many fans of different teams. It felt like I was in a wood-paneled cafeteria with all the customers looking at their personal devices. I did like how they have the sports pages up in front of the urinals.

Perhaps part of my melancholy right now is because of my experience at South Station, where before going to the bar I set up my "What Would You Ask Tom Brady?" sign.

It started off well. I particularly enjoyed watching the various branches of security in the station bicker in front of me, trying to decide if what I was doing was legal. Eventually a broad-shouldered, redheaded Boston policeman declared it was fine for me to sit there, as long as I made sure not to solicit any personal information or promise anyone any services or products. He didn't have anything he wanted to ask Tom Brady, but he did give me a laugh.

Overall, the travelers at South Station who stopped to talk to me had more variety to their questions than those at the

Olde Mistick Village outdoor mall. Several people wanted to know Brady's political affiliation and his views on various social issues. A couple of middle-aged women asked if Brady would marry them. One young man spent a great deal of time talking to me about Tom Brady's hair, in particular about how he never seemed to get "helmet head."

"Just ask him where he wants his statue," whispered one guy to me conspiratorially. "Does he want it at Gillette or at City Hall? He's getting a statue, for sure."

"Y'know Rocky Marciano, the boxer?" said another man. "Italian. Boston city kid. He quit at 49 and o. Never lost a title fight, and he got out at thirty-two years old. That's how to do it, Tommy. Quit while you're ahead. 'cause you're starting to slide. Thirty-two years old Rocky was. I met him. I say quit while you're ahead."

Then I spoke with two middle-aged men who were eager to talk.

The first was thirty-five years old and told me his name was Peter. He rattled off several questions right away, as if he'd been waiting for someone to ask him this. "Why does he get so frustrated all the time?" Peter said. "Why doesn't he take over as coach? He's been there long enough. They obviously screwed up the Welker situation. They knew what they had. I think we're going to lose today, too, to the Steelers. At least we have the Red Sox."

Then Peter paused, and he got more serious. "Maybe he could give me some money. Maybe play some catch. I'd probably also ask if he still loves his wife." He thought on this one and added: "Probably not."

The other guy, a heavy man with a thick Boston accent, came over and pulled up a chair, which is what I thought I had been hoping for — another middle-aged man to open up about his thoughts on the quarterback.

"Ask Brady what you do if you live in abject poverty," he

said. "There's no way out. I used to be bellboy at the Four Seasons. I was making fifty grand a year. Tips. Rock stars [pronounced *stahs*], movie stars. I left there in '89, and I haven't had a good job since."

"Why did you leave?"

"There's a very high turnover rate in that position. A lot of brown-nosing. I did it for two and a half years. It was time to try something else. And it's slow during the wintertime. One guy gives you a hundred bucks, another guy throws you fifty cents. And them bags are pretty heavy after a while."

"What do you think Tom Brady should do with all his money?"

"Well, we can send it all overseas to all the dying people over the world, but my father was an honorably discharged Purple Heart decorated Vietnam veteran, and he lived in the alleys of Harvard Ave in Allston for twenty years. You know where Harvard Ave is? All right then. Twenty years. I had him committed to Bridgewater three times. Put him in Pine Street. Court Street. JP VA. Tewksbury VA. Died like a dog on the floor of an ATM machine. Nothing I could do for him, because I didn't have any money. Give Tom Brady my number and have him give me a call. I could tell him a few stories."

"That's a sad story. I'm sorry about your dad."

"It's a very typical story. I'm not the only Irish kid who grew up in the projects with a sad story to tell. I heard what that guy said to you about Rocky Marciano. That's fine. A tough Boston Italian kid made good. But how do you quit while you're ahead when you never got nowhere?"

NOVEMBER 6 / 10:15 A.M.
MYSTIC, CONNECTICUT

Cold and rainy. I'm back at the house on the couch for the morning. I was thinking that for "Mystic Backyard Boats," I'll need to build a barn in the back. I guess I'll need to check with planning and zoning. I spent some time online searching for kits on how to build your own barn with only a drill and a circular saw. When that didn't get me very far, I got horizontal and reread some of Frederick Exley's *A Fan's Notes.*

Exley wrote the novel in 1968 from the perspective of a man who is a writer, a full-bore alcoholic, and obsessed with Frank Gifford, then the star running back of the New York Giants. Like me, the writer has a day job as an English teacher that has lost its luster. Is there any larger cliché?

Exley says: "Why did football bring me so to life? I can't say precisely. Part of it was my feeling that football was an island of directness in a world of circumspection. In football a man was asked to do a difficult and brutal job, and he either did it or got out. There was nothing rhetorical or vague about it; I chose to believe that it was not unlike the jobs which all men, in some sunnier past, had been called upon to do. It smacked of something old, something traditional, something unclouded by legerdemain and subterfuge. It had that kind of power over me, drawing me back with the force of something known, scarcely remembered, elusive as integrity—perhaps it was no more than the force of a forgotten childhood."

Exley goes on to explain how Americans (e.g., me) often confuse success with wisdom. Exley, as the narrator, goes to college with Frank Gifford at the University of Southern California in the early 1950s. Gifford is the ultimate Big Man on Campus, written of constantly in the student newspapers. Young Exley begins to hate him for all his success.

He finally sees Gifford at a hamburger joint and watches the star halfback until he walks up to pay the cashier. Exley confronts Gifford. He stares at the football star with a "hard, mocking, so-you're-the-big-shit? smile." Gifford in turn smiles back: kindly, apologetically. This disarms the narrator. After Gifford leaves, Exley thinks about their meeting. It seems that

Gifford felt sorry for not recognizing him, maybe even embarrassed by his own success—as if he understood his good fortune and was bashful for it; as if he were sorry not to be able to treat everyone properly, to not remember every person he'd met and who had been good to him. Perhaps Gifford was bashful about standing on the fortunate side of chance or aristocracy or plutocracy or nepotism or some other unearned advantage.

This is the same way people describe Tom Brady. This is apparently the grace with which he handled his early success, and how he still does, after now living under the public's microscope for a third of his life. As if writing directly to me, Exley describes his narrator as filled with a misplaced frustration that is actually about himself. Gifford isn't the jerk; he is. Exley realizes that he couldn't hate Gifford, though he wanted to at first. For Exley, Frank Gifford—the football player, the person—becomes a symbol for life's promise.

Later in *A Fan's Notes*, the narrator's future wife, aptly named Patience, asks: "What is this thing with you and Gifford—or whatever his name is?"

Exley tries to explain about how he sees parallels between the two of them, but that Gifford had begun "to represent to me the possible, had sustained for me the illusion that I could escape the bleak anonymity of life."

"I should think you'd despise him," Patience says. "Oh, maybe not despise him. Envy him to the point of disliking him immensely."

"Despise him?" Exley says. "But you don't understand at all. Not at all! He may be the only fame I'll ever have!"

That's exactly what I've been trying to explain to Hoss and Lenny. Tom Brady is going to the Super Bowl this year. He is going to grab all the rookies and the injured and the replacements and the undrafted free agents and swing them on his back, and roll on past Peyton Manning and the Denver Broncos. For one final fantastic underdog fourth-quarter come-back, Tom Brady is going to win it all, grab that fourth ring, and ascend to the throne of the best there ever was. And I am behind him. I have been behind him. I am an investor. I will share that glory.

And you know what else? One day soon I'm going to walk down some hallway, and Tom Brady is going to see me and nod his head. We'll walk toward each other, knock a fist bump, and keep right on rollin'.

"Hey, Rich."

"Hey, Tom."

NOVEMBER 7 / 1:10 P.M.
MYSTIC, CONNECTICUT

Uncle Frank sent me a handwritten postcard on which he had glued a photograph of a cormorant standing on a piling beside the Hudson River, with a bloody eel in its mouth: "The more one thinks about Brady, the more one welcomes your mission, because you are going to solve the great mystery about him, right? Like you almost solved the great mystery of whether the double-crested cormorant is analogous to a hum-mingbird sipping nectar from a beautiful flower. It is weird, isn't it? That such a beautiful man exists on a field with so many animals. As I am watching Brady play, I get the sense that I am watching a brilliant as well as a beautiful athlete. But he isn't brilliant in anything but football, and in that case he's probably more intuitive than brilliant."

Moving on to the address side of the postcard, Uncle Frank scrunched in: "So that makes him in a weird way unique. I know of no other participant in any other sport where there is such a glaring difference between a player and those around him. The whole thing is peculiar. Like that famous classical Greco-Roman statue of the naked killer with a Trojan helmet and short sword. What is one supposed to say to him?"

He signed it: "Anyway, good luck. You will get your chance. Frank."

NOVEMBER 8 / 11:25 A.M.
EN ROUTE FROM PROVIDENCE TO DETROIT

On the plane. Over the last month I received a few brief responses from various public relations people at the University of Michigan, but no interviews or press pass or special access or really anything came out of our correspondence. They did write me back at least, so perhaps the Michigan staff is not on Brady's batch of contacts for his crazy list—or maybe if I'm lucky I haven't made the list yet.

As I tried to connect to anyone at "Big Blue," I found out that a friend of mine has a brother-in-law named Brian Movalson, who is a leader in the sports business, especially in television and video games. Only a couple of years older than I am, Brian is now in charge of all the University of Oregon's media rights for IMG, one of the world's leading sports marketing agencies. He got his start at the University of Michigan, where he was a student in sports management. Brian squeezed me in for a phone call only a few hours before a prime-time Oregon football game.

"You talked to Matt Cassel?" he said. "Great guy! Our two families vacationed together in the Turks and Caicos!"

Brian had a couple of ideas about whom to contact at Michigan, what I should see, and he confirmed that Stacey James of the Patriots is the best way to contact Brady. He did not think athletes have any kind of crazy list.

"But sometimes you have to talk to seven people to get to one," Brian said. "You need the guy that cuts Tom Brady's hair. You just got to keep trying. Maybe go right to his old coach at

Michigan, Lloyd Carr? Listen, Brady's a premier athlete. Isn't he one of the top ten highest-paid athletes in the world? A gigantic marketable asset. He stands out. He's got the boyish good looks, the good luck, the Super Bowls. The whole package. There are only a few athletes in his class—maybe Derek Jeter, LeBron James. Peyton Manning will endorse anything; he likes that sort of spotlight. But Brady's been very selective with his endorsements. And who he talks to."

NOVEMBER 8 / 10:30 P.M.
ANN ARBOR, MICHIGAN

I checked my e-mail—and a completion! This tossed back from the Pressman Stacey James: "Sure. You may come to a press conference, although I don't know if that will be Tuesday or Thursday at this point."

NOVEMBER 9 / 2:15 P.M.
ANN ARBOR, MICHIGAN

I'm sitting on a hill before such a vast expanse of tailgating that my only point of comparison is footage I've seen of Woodstock. I've never been to a Big Ten football game. I have never seen anything like this in my life.

I can see acres—miles—of tents, trucks, buses, RVs, cars, and people crowded on the fields and parking lots and far up into a distant golf course. To my right I can see the stadium, a large brick coliseum known here simply as "the Big House," built in 1927, which is the largest sports stadium in the United States, college or professional. A massive blue sign with a huge bold yellow block "M" towers over this part of town. The colors are officially maize and blue. I can smell cigar smoke, keg beer, barbecue, potato salad, marijuana, and autumn leaves. Little kids throw footballs and roll themselves down hills; college kids cradle red Solo cups and toss maize-and-blue sandbags toward cornholes; middle-aged revelers sway to music bouncing from their truck radios; and older couples in straw hats lounge in seats before tableclothed spreads that would not be out of place at a garden wedding. Maize and blue are everywhere, dotted only occasionally by the bold red and white of the Nebraska Cornhuskers, the Wolverines' opponent today. Far in the distance I see a Star Wars storm trooper with a Michigan cape wielding a giant Michigan flag and sprinting down a hill, weaving and waving between maize-and-blue tents and a school bus painted with the Michigan winged-helmet design on the roof of which a dozen partiers dance the cancan.

Before I got here I read about Tom Brady's experience at the University of Michigan, which is where the legend of this star quarterback as a scrappy underdog began. It was here he earned the nickname "the Comeback Kid."

When eighteen-year-old Brady arrived on campus from California in 1995, he was one of seven quarterbacks in camp. He made the team but was redshirted. The next year he played in just two games. Tom Brady's first-ever pass as a Wolverine was during mop-up time in a fourth-quarter rout of the UCLA Bruins at the Big House. A UCLA linebacker easily picked off Brady's short pass and returned the ball for six points and the only Bruins touchdown of the day.

The following year, his sophomore year of eligibility, Brady was in the hunt for the starting job but lost out to senior Brian Griese—the son of Miami Dolphins legend Bob Griese. Brady considered transferring back home to the University of California–Berkeley to get playing time, but he was swayed in part by the school's sports counselor and, as the story goes, a drive to prove himself, to not quit. The Wolverines with Griese under center went on to an undefeated season and the college's first national championship (shared with Nebraska) in nearly half a century.

In 1998, his junior year of eligibility, Brady took over as the starter. After a dubious opening pair of games, he led Big Blue to a respectable 10–3 finish, tying for the Big Ten conference championship. He threw a game-winning touchdown late in the fourth quarter to beat Arkansas in the Citrus Bowl.

Michigan coach Lloyd Carr did not, however, hand Brady the starting job for his senior year, even though his teammates elected him captain. The University of Michigan had now groomed Drew Henson, a local Michigan high school hero and a two-sport athlete who already had a multimillion dollar contract with the New York Yankees whenever he got tired of playing football. Carr decided that Brady would play the first quarter, Henson would play the second, and then he would choose at halftime who had the hot hand and would finish the game. People say that Brady did not complain. He dug deeper.

(As it happens, six years earlier, at a small Division III school in New Jersey, I was coming back my junior year from a bout of mononucleosis that knocked me out from playing lacrosse the year before, when I was the starting goalie. In a similar situation at a far smaller scale, my coach decided that I would split time as the starter with a younger talent. Did I dig deeper? Did I put the team before my own needs? I quit the sport.)

By midway through the season, Brady earned the job outright and led the team to a 10–2 record. He earned his team's MVP award for the season and led a barn-burning win at the Orange Bowl. Tom Brady played his best game of his college career on this biggest stage, throwing for four touchdowns, completing 74 percent of his passes, and setting a Michigan bowl record of 369 yards in the air. It was the most productive game by any quarterback in the history of Michigan football. During this Orange Bowl, Michigan was down two touchdowns at two separate stages of the game. On the first play in overtime, Brady rolled out from a blitz and zinged the ball to his tight end, who lumbered right down into the end zone.

I've spent the last couple of hours touring all the side streets and parking lots and fields and interviewing gameday tailgaters about what they would ask Tom Brady. This was his undergraduate campus—where he had a 3.3 GPA—which was, as it happens, exactly my own college GPA. Brady earned a bachelor of general studies with a business and psychology emphasis. I earned a bachelor of arts with a major in psychology. We both chose careers different from our undergraduate studies.

One family tailgating beside the Big House had a maize and blue 1960s Volkswagen bug customized for the current Michigan coach, Brady Hoke, hand-painted with the name "Hoke's Wagon." I spoke with Teri, the daughter of the vw's owner, and her friend, Samantha. Both of them were at Michigan when Brady was a student-athlete. They saw him a couple of times at house parties.

I asked Teri: "Any stories you can share?"

"Not that she's going to tell you on tape," laughed Samantha. "And not with her dad right there."

"No, he was an average guy," Teri said. "Which even of itself is amazing."

"Being normal," said the friend. "They all are. The athletes. Pretty normal."

Like most everyone else I've spoken to, the two women explained about how young Tom Brady and current Tom Brady represent so well the values of Michigan: the hard work, the humility, and the respect for football tradition. When they see the Patriots on television, they see first their most favorite and most accomplished Wolverine—even if he was only very

good, not *amazing*, at the Big House. Teri told me how she now owns a Patriots number-twelve jersey.

As I made my way into the tailgating fields, everyone knew well the story of Brady's years at Michigan, about Drew Henson, about how Brady struggled, about how he "grew up a lot in Ann Arbor," as one tailgater put it, and about how he saved his best for last in that Orange Bowl. All had also watched carefully the video of the speech a couple of months ago that Tom Brady had delivered before the current team of Wolverines, when he stopped in the afternoon before this year's preseason game against the Detroit Lions.

One guy, holding his half-eaten burger, bent my ear hard and loud: "There's a reason why Tom Brady told those players that his greatest individual accomplishment was being voted captain at Michigan. Because it's Michigan! You could say, okay, well, Alabama is a great team. You got your Big Twelve in Texas. Or you got some of these other schools. But it's Michigan! That means something. This guy won Super Bowls, MVPs. You would think, aw, his greatest accomplishment is Super Bowl MVP. No! It was captain at Michigan. Everybody said he was too skinny. Everybody said he wasn't good enough."

The guy continued, shouting over his friends who wanted me to ask Brady about where he gets his confidence: "I would ask Tom Brady how he feels about the fact that even though there were so many Wolverine fans, so few of them felt like he could *not* do it. But not me! I felt like Tom Brady was *The Man*. And how did he feel after that, when no one but me believed in him? He got to the NFL and held clipboards and never bitched. He took his time and was professional. Never bitched. Not one time! Then he got his chance, and he never looked back. He knew it. And if you really and truly watched that Orange Bowl, there's no way you could *not* have faith in him."

The tailgaters with whom I spent the most time were a collection of men in their forties and fifties, guys who have done well for themselves, as evidenced by their five-star trailer, which opened up to a professional grill, a wide-screen TV, and a bar with multiple taps. A couple of these guys have been involved in the alumni association. I first approached one of them, named Ryan, because he wore a Michigan Tom Brady jersey with the Orange Bowl patch. They were all excited to talk to me, because they had been discussing Brady at length an hour or so before I arrived.

"He was such a warrior when he was here," Ryan said. "He was nothing but a warrior. You look at some of our greatest comebacks. A warrior. The run game kept breaking down. And he would bring us back. Just a phenomenal guy. You never heard any transgression against him, either, about not going to class or drinking off campus, or whatever. I never understood why he was so underrated in the draft. I believed in him, though. And I'll never forget how poised he was in that interview after the win over Notre Dame his senior year. Such a leader he was, and he so loved Michigan. And to see him address the team *this year* before Notre Dame—"

"That was goose bumps," said Ryan's college roommate.

"I was at that game against Penn State, *at* Penn State," said another friend, named Philip. "We were down something like ten points in the fourth quarter, and I had very good seats, and he ran up and down that Michigan sideline saying: 'Don't hang your heads. We are going to win this game. Do not hang your heads. We are going to win this game!' And he went out and willed that win."

"That's right," said Ryan.

"That's true," said the roommate. "We were all there. You could hear it."

"That meant a lot to us," Ryan said.

"My question to Tom Brady," said Philip, "is how often do

you go to pee-wee leagues and high schools and tell those kids what kind of sacrifice you had to make to get where you are? Not to live the dream necessarily, but to have fulfillment in your athleticism. You had tremendous natural talent. *Have* tremendous talent. What does he say to a young kid who has dreams of being Tom Brady? Or to that kid's parents who have aspirations of him being Tom Brady? When do you pull back?"

A fourth friend, named Evan, said: "He's a great football player, but is he a great photographer, is he a great lawyer, is he a great CPA? No. Everyone's great in his own aspect. And I guess it's the religious side of me, but we're all equal, but with our own talents. We're just different."

"Whatever, grandmom," said Ryan to Evan. "There isn't a person standing in these fields that's equal to Tom Brady."

8:45 P.M.

Sitting at a restaurant downtown after the game. I walked with the tide of sad Michigan boosters back up State Street and found this place, occupied by maybe half Michigan fans, a quarter Nebraska fans, and a quarter of people who thought they were getting away from football on Saturday but chose the wrong restaurant.

I watched the game from Row 93, nearly at the top of the Big House, at the corner of the end zone, surrounded by Nebraska boosters. I bought a maize and blue scarf, partly out of necessity because it was so blustery cold, and I sat next to an older couple from outside Omaha. I enjoyed their quiet company, and occasionally on a few plays we consulted on what had happened. It was a sloppy football game. The Michigan quarterback got sacked continually and never got the message to get rid of the ball faster. Nebraska won in the end. Still ringing in my ear is a young man who sat a few seats away and shouted, almost every two minutes, "Goooo Huskers!" He bellowed this same call often without any prompting of a play or other stimulus. He grew hoarser as the game went on, but this did not stop his occasional cry, like a cow in pain, like a cuckoo clock, and this gave my new Nebraska friends and me a good point to smile about.

I loved listening to the bands during the game, the school songs for both sides, and I liked the relatively small Jumbotron, which forced me to focus on the happenings on the field. In the first quarter the stadium announced that attendance today was 112,204 people. This is the 250th game in a row that this stadium has packed in over 100,000 fans. The Michigan Wolverines have won more football games over their long history than any other program in the country. I remain in awe of the type of young man that Tom Brady must've been at eighteen years old.

Tom, where did you find the confidence and ambition to visit this campus as a high school kid and think: Yep, right here is where I want to be the starting quarterback?

Super Bowls never have as many people in the stands as regularly pile into a Big Ten, Big Blue festival that is the big game, the contest for Caesar, at the Big House. The capacity of Gillette Stadium in Foxborough is less than sixty-nine thousand people. I've heard Brady talk about that—about how the crowds and pressure in the NFL never really affected him as much. He had led his team to victories before the hollering mobs at Michigan.

Tom, I'm going to pretend to be tight end Shawn Thompson and cut on a slant to catch that winning overtime TD against Alabama in the Orange Bowl. When you recall that day, do you hear the trumpets, the drums,

the Michigan fight song, the "Hail! to the victors valiant"?
Do you remember that play, after you snapped that
football? Do you remember how it felt when it left your
fingertips?

NOVEMBER 11 / 10:15 P.M.
MYSTIC, CONNECTICUT

Felt sluggish on my run this morning. I don't want to clock the distance with the car, for fear my loop will turn out to be only two miles.

My parents have offered us their old Volvo station wagon for when we sell the van. A Volvo station wagon. It has fold-down booster seats for kids. It's the safest car you can buy in the case of an accident, and thus is the preferred car of nearly all the wives of Connecticut insurance salesmen. Automatic transmission. Lisa likes the heated driver seat for the winter.

Teaching *The Old Man and the Sea* today. The more I read this novel as I grow older, the more I understand Santiago in his boat alone, looking back on his life, claiming to no longer be interested in competitions or chasing after women or conflict of any kind, and yet he can't help going deep for the biggest fish of his life. And he can't help comparing himself to a baseball player, the great Joe DiMaggio, and wondering how the star center fielder's endurance of pain relates to his own.

I'll bet neither Joe DiMaggio or Santiago or Tom Brady suffered as I do, having to sell their vintage van in order to drive around in a reliable, safe Volvo station wagon—and not even the old, cool, clunky kind of Volvo, but one that looks practically new, maintained dutifully by grandparents at their local Volvo dealership. Oh, the pain. The cross I bear.

I'm nervous, like before a job interview. I'm keeping my eyes down. Maybe it's because despite a lot of searching around on the Internet I still do not know what Pressman James looks like. Was I supposed to check in with someone? When exactly is Tom Brady going to come out? All the people here seem relaxed, seated, chatting, or working on their computers or phones. They all seem to know what is going to happen next. I have this feeling that someone is going to ask me a question or tap me on the shoulder to expose me, or that Tom Brady himself is going to ask *me* something when he comes out. Which will be when exactly?

To get in here, Pressman James told me over e-mail to go to ticket booth seventeen. A man found my name on a list and, when writing out the press pass, looked up and asked me: "What outlet?"

"What outlet?" I repeated.

"Yeah, what media outlet?"

What media outlet was I? Well, er, none really. I gave him the name of the college where I teach. He wrote it on the pass under the Patriots logo. I walked up to the Gillette Stadium gate, which is at the level of the field. I showed my pass to security. I didn't ask the guard where to go, because I was afraid he'd change his mind about letting me in. I walked through the towering corridor, past the stands, and leaned down to feel the turf. I stood on the edge behind the end zone. I stepped onto the green. Desperate to sprint across the entire length of the field—to pretend to be Julian Edelman on a punt return slicing a few sharp cuts and then going the distance across the midfield logo all the way to . . . the . . . house —I realized dozens of constant-feed cameras surely would be watching me. That one act, although so satisfying, would ruin any chance for my catch and conversation with Tom. I was also wearing dress shoes. I would slip and wipe out.

Back toward the gate, I saw a sign on a door for press and walked in, trying to seem as confident as possible. I walked down a short hallway with offices on both sides, a couple labeled with a particular organization, such as the *Boston Globe*, and one large area unlabeled, with open cubbies for general use by reporters. In a small foyer were free stacks of *Patriots Football Weekly* and assembled paperwork about the upcoming game, the history of the Patriots, and all of the season's stats in exhaustive spreadsheet tables stapled in thick booklets. I gathered each item of free material, pretending I barely wanted it, and then walked into the conference room where I am now. Desks line both side walls. There aren't as many chairs as I expected, forty-eight total, but there are seven big film rigs aimed at the podium.

I took this seat in the back row and am trying to blend in. This is a "Brady presser," according to the lingo I'm hearing. I'm slightly overdressed: no one else is wearing a sweater vest, for example, but I don't think I'm conspicuously far above the mean.

One older male reporter and a younger female one are chatting in the seats in front of me. She's talking about her recent experience covering the Red Sox World Series. "The champagne in the locker room. It totally stinks! It reeks!"

"Oh yeah," says the older guy, "I've been there many times. I was in the locker room for all the Super Bowls, too. Imagine if we did that after writing a really good piece. I've just won a local Emmy! Blast the champagne all over everything!"

Walking in now are a few people I recognize from various NFL and Patriots shows and radio programs, including one man dressed in a suit who is younger than he looks on television. He seems to have on makeup. I never would've expected this from his demeanor on TV, but he's a total potty mouth. "Hey, asshole!" he shouts across to a cameraman friend, shattering the tone of the room. He asks a fellow reporter, "What fucking week of the NFL is this, anyway? I'm just in from Atlanta. Fucking Georgia Dome."

There are about twenty-four people in the room now. A lot of empty chairs. Someone laid out a whole table of sandwiches in the foyer. I really want one. But I don't dare.

A woman in her forties with an intelligent face says to another reporter: "Covering the Patriots is like covering the Nixon administration."

Wait, is that guy over there the Pressman Stacey James? He seems to be managing things, going in and out of the door to the right of the stage and also through some door to the left of the Dunkin' Donuts backdrop behind the podium. Should I introduce myself?

"Here we go, boys," says somebody, and just like that, here

he is. Tom Brady is walking in the room. Tom Brady in person. Tom Brady ten yards away.

7:45 P.M. / MYSTIC, CONNECTICUT

I still can't believe today! Lisa and my friends have made fun of me, saying I must have some sort of homoerotic crush on Brady. I really don't think I do, but I have to admit, he sure is a good-looking man! He was tall, which I did expect, but had more of a basketball player's build. Perhaps because of his cheeks freshly shaved and red, presumably from practicing outside, I couldn't stop looking at his white teeth. They shimmered. His smile was a toothpaste advertisement—and that chin cleft looked deeper and more distinct in person. His face seemed actually *less* real off the screen, like a comic book version of a John Travolta–inspired superhero. In sweats. He wore a New England Patriots striped pom-pom hat, too, which only made him appear more rugged by the contrast of the goofy cap, like when Beyoncé or Kate Upton wears some dime-store foam-front trucker baseball hat, rendering her still more gorgeous.

As with every other press conference Brady has ever held, the content of his responses to any given question in a variety of forms can be boiled down to the following: (1) the upcoming opponent is a very good team; (2) [fill in name of teammate] is a really hard worker, but we can all execute better; or (3) [smile] that's really the coach's/management's/doctor's decision.

One reporter asked this afternoon, for example: "Tom, can you talk about the Carolina defense and what they bring to the table there? They're red hot right now."

"Yep, they've won five straight," Brady says. He nods kindly, as if this is a very good question, as if he hasn't answered a question like this nine hundred times. "They're a great team defense. I mean, everything. They got every stat. Every category. Third down. Red area. Sacks. They turn it over. They got it all. I mean, they're one of the best defenses in the league. So we have to play really well. I think our execution has to be at its best. It'll be fun. It's Monday night. It's getting later in the year, the games are more and more important. And we'll see what we can do."

The reporters chimed in smoothly and somehow didn't talk over each other. No one raised hands. No women asked questions. One journalist finished with: "Thirteen years in the NFL, Monday night football still excite you, in and of itself?"

"Sure, yeah, no question. It's fun. Now with Thursday night football and there's Saturday night football. But Monday night football is always pretty cool, and especially when you play a really good team on Monday night football. I mean, it's a fun night. It's November. You feel the weather changing out there. So it's when the most important games are, you want to be playing in the biggest moments."

Brady paused and said, "All right, thank you, guys."

He exited stage right, tall and lanky. He walked out the door, carrying himself—whether real or affected—as a bit embarrassed to have everyone watching him. His press conference lasted seven minutes.

The reporters continued sitting around, chatting, and a few people moved to the door where Brady had exited. The guy who I thought was Pressman James turned out not to be. I decided not to leave yet. I sat around with the rest of the reporters to see what was going to happen next. The minutes ticked by. No one seemed to be going anywhere.

Then the door opened and every single person in the room stood up quickly and went toward it. In my correspondence with Pressman James, we'd never talked about anything else besides the press conference. I didn't want to ruin a future opportunity. This was my chance to show that I'm trustworthy and *not* a nutball. But, then again, all the reporters were going somewhere where I surely wanted to go. I couldn't help it. I stayed in the middle of the group. We walked across a hallway and then into the locker room. Into the New England Patriots locker room!

The first person I saw was one of the Patriots running backs, and then his naked butt as he slung off his towel to change by his chair. That was embarrassing. It turned out there was a lot more skin than I expected, even with all the press people in there. Guys strolled to and from the showers and a workout space in another room. The locker area itself was much tidier than I imagined. A massive Patriots logo decorated the gray carpet, and all the lockers were open and neat. It certainly didn't smell like any locker room I've ever been associated with, and players seem to keep very little in their open cubbies. No combination locks, no metal clanking doors, no crumpled-up Gatorade cans or banana peels or swirls of ace bandages or sweaty jockstraps. Each "locker" is really a section of dark wood finished shelves, so the space seemed more like a Fortune 500 boardroom or even a library — it was as if this was a stage locker room set up for the media's benefit and then the guys actually had a real place in the back where they could put their dirty crap in piles and sit around to unwrap their tape and clip their toenails.

Tom, after a particularly muddy practice, do you guys have to take off all your stuff and leave it in the hallway before you can go into the locker room?

I tried to stay cool and look like I belonged in there, but I couldn't figure out exactly what the rules were. The reporters and cameramen milled around and talked to each other as the players and coaches walked through or to their lockers. Other than Tom Brady himself and Rob Gronkowski, I saw nearly every player on the team. But not everyone talked to the press. All of a sudden a clump of reporters would encircle a player at his locker, while another equally relevant player would be changing right next to him and no one would ask him any questions. Always a step behind, I followed the little rushes around the locker room. I reached my audio recorder toward offensive lineman Logan Mankins to get his comments on why he preferred playing Sundays at 4:25 rather than a Monday night game, how he spent the bye week, and so on. I recorded Patriots defensive back Devin McCourty answering questions about how they will try to contain the Panthers' mobile quarterback Cam Newton. Mostly, though, I stood as close to Tom Brady's locker as I could without, I hoped, appearing too creepy or obvious. I took notes on a legal pad. I was the only journalist writing anything longhand. I sketched Brady's locker surreptitiously.

At one point Coach Bill Belichick almost slammed into me. He was hurrying through with his head down, chewing gum hard, avoiding eye contact with everyone. He had his whistle twirled around his fingers. I didn't know if he was going to avoid me, or if I should avoid him, and we both went the same way for a moment, almost banged into each other, but then he stuttered right and escaped. I tried to smile at him, but he kept his head down. I'm teaching tutorials now on *Moby-Dick*, so I immediately thought of how Stubb, the second mate, dreamed of being kicked by Ahab with his

whalebone leg. In the dream an old merman tells him: "You were kicked by a great man . . . It's an honor!" I wish I'd given a quick fake to the left and Belichick steamrolled right over me.

Eventually the journalists began to move out of the locker room. I followed. Back in the press conference room, I packed up and left. Better to leave before Pressman James found me or before I did anything that would get me on the crazy list. I did, however, snag a free sandwich, and I did go out and stand by the field a little longer. When I took a few more steps into the end zone, I caught the eye of a photographer shooting from the open corridor. He gave me a nod and smile as if to say, *Yep, I did that my first time, too.*

NOVEMBER 14 / 9:15 P.M.
MYSTIC, CONNECTICUT

I watched video clips of the locker room press section on the website, and I can see a few fingers of my right arm and my digital recorder during the Logan Mankins interview.

The van made it to Foxborough and home without any problem. But it felt hollow without Ruby in there.

At one point when I was in the locker room I overhead Ryan Mallett, the six-foot-six backup quarterback for the Patriots, speaking informally to two female reporters, one a newspaper journalist and one a television host. Mallett is in the process of growing a beard and wore thick black-rimmed glasses and cozy slippers. He joked about how the only thing anybody ever wanted to ask him about was Tom Brady. "As if he and I have dinner together every night!" The two reporters laughed and said that people they meet always first ask them about Brady, too.

The three of them discussed an incident a few years ago when a reporter in the locker room asked Brady about the season opener, and Brady said: "Yeah, start drinking early.

Get nice and rowdy. It's a 4:15 game, a lot of time to get lubed up. Come out here and cheer for [the] home team."

Within one hour Pressman James clarified that Brady meant water. He "wants everyone to drink a lot of water, stay hydrated. Drink responsibly."

The three joked about the incident, a rare Brady slip. Mallett said it showed how Brady was a regular guy.

Listening to Mallett and the two reporters chat, while I was gawking at Brady's locker, I was reminded once again of how much of a cliché I am. Headline: "Middle-Aged Men Who Are Officially Fascinated with Superstar Tom Brady Hits the One Million Mark."

After I got home last night I wrote to Pressman James to thank him for letting me come.

He responded a couple of hours later, at 10:59 p.m.: "I assumed that was you. Sorry that I didn't get a chance to say hello for an introduction."

NOVEMBER 16 / 7:25 A.M.
MYSTIC, CONNECTICUT

Last night I had a dream that I called Larry Bird in the middle of the night. I don't know why I called or what I had to say, but he was really pissed off at me. In the dream he was wearing his Boston Celtics shirt with pajama bottoms, ranting about fans and privacy.

NOVEMBER 17 / 3:20 P.M.
MYSTIC, CONNECTICUT

"I looks like we're just five again today."

"It's too cold to play football."

"Can I play steady QB? I'm hurt."

"With what?"

"I've pulled my sports-groin."

"What's that?"

"It's what Danny Amendola has. Athletic pubalgia."

"Pubalgia?"

"You want me to show you?"

"Please don't."

"How's your stalking going?"

"I am *not* stalking. But it's not looking good."

"What are you talking about?! Did he tell you all about how he got into the locker room?!"

"It's true. That was amazing, truly amazing. But I don't think I'm going to meet him in the end."

"It's okay if you fail, you know. We'll still love you."

"Maybe after the season he'll meet me. I'm still going to keep trying. Maybe Brady will admire my persistence. I feel like I can't just quit now, y'know? I always quit stuff."

"What is it with us all?" Munro said. "The persistence crap. The *you can get it if you really want it* load. The American Dream. It's just not the way it works."

"Whoa, easy, counselor."

"No, seriously," said Munro, who works as an urban planner. "Can I bring up something here? I've been thinking about this a lot recently."

"Alert! Philosophy major prepareth to pontificate!"

"Can we start playing, please?" objected Kevin the librarian. "I'm freezing."

Munro held the football like a gavel, undaunted. "What I want to bring up is that privilege begets privilege. Sure there are exceptions, like, say, Barack Obama, but on the whole—and, yeah, maybe sports are probably better than a whole lot of other professions, maybe the fastest way to rise—"

"An even playing field."

"Good one. But, well, what did Brady grow up with? Did he grow up in a sports family?"

"I know he's got three older sisters who were really good at sports. I read that they all earned college scholarships in softball or soccer. And I guess he used to play a lot of golf with his dad. Brady played baseball before football."

"Can we kick off, please?" Kevin said. "I need to start running around. This is how you get varicose veins."

"So if he's playing golf every week, he's a rich kid," said Munro.

"I think he was, actually," I said. "Relatively, anyway. He went to a private school south of San Fran. Lisa grew up near there, and she said that's where a lot of the wealthy kids went."

"Didn't Brady have personal coaches growing up?"

"Yeah, he had his own private quarterback coach in high school. A man who coached at a local community college then stayed Brady's personal coach until he died a couple years ago. I think that guy—or maybe it was the high school coach or his dad—helped Brady make a recruitment video to send to colleges."

"My point exactly. Sure, plenty of star quarterbacks maybe come from poverty, but it's not an even playing field. Just like Olympians or whatever, everyone does not start at the same place or have the same resources for training or getting noticed. Whether it's Harvard or the NFL or Goldman Sachs."

"Munro, are you getting fired?"

"He's getting shut out of a will."

"No and no. I'm just saying that we're not all born standing on the same starting line. And I'm not talking just about genetics. The line consistently shifts no matter what your goals. Look at it this way, about your man crush: Is there anybody as good as Brady in football?"

"Peyton Manning. Who's the son of Archie Manning, a former NFL QB himself. And his brother Eli for the Giants—"

"Again, my point exactly."

"Brady was drafted in the sixth round," I said. "He's an underdog. He's had to scrape."

"That's the narrative. But I bet it's not the whole truth. Look at it this way. Do you think any amount of scraping or hard work is going to help you meet Tom Brady? No. We're brought up: *Don't quit! You can do it, little train!* That's our problem. We're brought up that hard work equals results, no matter what you want to do. It's not always true. It's probably even *rarely* true. So we end up all feeling like failures. Because we didn't try hard enough. Maybe what you want isn't even something acquirable by hard work or practice or study in the first place. Some things you can simply not get by the force of will. Sometimes it's dumb luck. And not just the luck of birth or genes or whatever. Only successful people, people who have arrived, think free will and hard work have the majority stake in anything."

"Ladies, puh-lease. Munro! My free will is for you to kick off the goddamn ball. Or I'm going to kick off yours!"

NOVEMBER 18 / 9:35 P.M.
MYSTIC, CONNECTICUT

At Pier 27. Tom Brady has been playing well tonight, as has the Carolina Panthers QB Cam Newton. I like watching Monday night football here because all the televisions have the same game on. Dolphins Guy is at his stool at the bar, as is Chicken Little at the other end. But few of the other regulars came out tonight. Steelers Alley is quiet. Loud Brady Lady and her husband didn't come, nor did Nick Name, Dr. No-No, or even Gangly John.

This afternoon I drove to the University of Massachusetts to interview Sean Glennon, the author of four books on the Patriots, including most recently *Tom Brady vs. the NFL: The Case for Football's Greatest Quarterback*, in which he argues that Brady is the best to ever play the position. In the book Glennon goes through all the biggies on Mount Passmore —Unitas, Montana, Manning, and Brady—as well as other greats like Staubach, Marino, and Favre. He writes too about some of the lesser-known but hugely influential early quarterbacks like Sammy Baugh and Sid Luckman. (Shalom, Mr. Luckman!) Glennon uses comparative statistics and general narrative descriptions to try to prove why Brady is the absolute king of them all.

Glennon starts the book by comparing Tom Brady to Peyton Manning: "There will never come a day when Tom Brady's name isn't connected with Peyton Manning's. Not ever."

Brady's team has beaten Peyton's far more often, but Glennon points out that this is a flawed gauge, because the Patriots have usually had better defenses, and these head-to-head matchups are really a small fraction of two very long careers. Glennon instead focuses on the fact Manning had a dome at his home field for most of his career, which is conducive to the passing game. More important, although Manning has four league MVPs, Brady has two more Super Bowl rings and a much higher winning percentage during the season —and even more so during the postseason. Brady has the most playoff wins in history, while Manning has lost more games than he's won in his postseason starts. Glennon argues that Brady has also statistically performed much better in all these postseason games. When Brady won his Super Bowls it's been mostly on his shoulders. In his second Super Bowl win, against the Carolina Panthers actually, he led another fourth-quarter drive just like for his first trophy, to put his kicker in a position to nail the game-winner with seconds left. When Brady lost his last two biggest games more recently, it's been his defense that hasn't held in the closing minutes. Brady has had them in the position to win each time with only a few minutes to go. Glennon argues that by contrast, Manning in his loss to the Saints in Super Bowl XLIV "inarguably cost his team its last chance" when he threw a pick-six late in the fourth quarter.

This season might forever alter the Brady-Manning debate, because the dome argument is out the window, so to speak, since Manning is now in his second year at Denver, and the numbers he's putting up this fall are so extravagant that the Broncos signal caller is on pace to beat all the records set by Brady and his offense from the Patriots' 2007 undefeated season.

One thing I'm conscious of as I'm watching this game at Pier 27 tonight is the Panthers' third-year quarterback Cam Newton, an extraordinary athlete, who is six foot five and nearly 250 pounds. He's been avoiding sacks from the Patriots and running downfield, faking out linebackers and making the whole defense look silly.

"We don't have a single player who can stop Newton," wailed Mr. Little. "Belichick refuses to draft a true pass rusher, so we look like the junior varsity team with Newton there. This game is over. We're done. Say goodbye to making the playoffs."

Cam Newton is African American. There isn't a single black quarterback in Sean Glennon's book. The only black quarterback in the Hall of Fame, Warren Moon—who wore number one like Cam Newton—broke a few racial barriers, and he's in the top ten for several all-time records, but he never led his team to the Super Bowl, and over his total career he won only one more game than he lost. A couple of black quarterbacks have brought their teams to the biggest game, to the largest spectator event in America, but only Doug Williams, playing for the Washington Redskins, won the Super Bowl.

So why are there so few elite black quarterbacks? Most positions on the professional football field are now dominated by African American players. Where is the African American Tom Brady? Cam doesn't seem like he's quite there yet, but he sure looks like a Hall of Famer tonight. He has been passing accurately, and his ability to run so aggressively downfield adds an entirely different dimension that Brady cannot offer.

Would I find Tom Brady as compelling—would I be so interested in his rise and fall, feel so connected, if he were a black man? Would New England sports fans idolize him so much? Did Boston Celtics fans idolize Larry Bird more than Bill Russell? Even today, do white quarterbacks get a certain underlying, subconscious support that black quarterbacks do not? When Michael Vick of the Philadelphia Eagles was getting pummeled by defensemen week after week a couple of years ago, many suggested that referees were keeping their unnecessary-roughness flags in their pockets not because he was a mobile quarterback, but because he was a black quarterback. What if that's even partly true? Likely the root of the lack of star black quarterbacks in the NFL is connected to the lack of black head coaches at all levels—and to the early high school and college coaches of any race who steer young black quarterback hopefuls to every other position.

I met Sean Glennon at a University of Massachusetts cafeteria. He was an exceptionally personable guy, has a ten-year-old son, and is not the type of statistics wonk that I expected. Yet he also had a ridiculous amount of NFL history at the tip of his tongue. In the kindest of ways, for example, he buried my theory that beards make quarterbacks lose, pointing out that both Ben Roethlisberger and Aaron Rodgers wore beards on the way to win their recent Super Bowls.

"I don't think we're going to get the Elway-type exit for Brady," Sean told me. "You listen to the things that Brady says. It used to be he wanted to play another five years. Then he wants to play until he's forty—now he wants to play *past* forty. He just seems like one of those guys who is going to play until they tell him he can't anymore. Which seems more the rule rather than the exception. So say the Patriots were to pull it together and win the Super Bowl this year. I don't see him riding off into the sunset. Even if they win them back to back. I think he's probably going to play until he's not welcome in the building. It's kind of awful that so many of them go out that way, isn't it?

"This guy's thirty-six years old," Sean continued. "And things are going to get ugly around here quick. I know you're a Patriots fan, but I'm sure you know that. When he goes, and particularly when Belichick goes, there's going to be some lean years. Because, man, for Patriots fans, the expectations are set so high."

Sean wasn't sure if Brady has actually begun his decline yet, if "the inevitable is upon us." At the start of this season, Brady and Belichick's offense was based on having two star tight ends. But then there was the tragic release of Hernandez, the slow healing of Gronk, the loss of Welker, the awkward adjustment of all these new young receivers, and now all the significant injuries on both sides of the ball.

"It does seem to be clicking, though, with Gronk fully back," he said. "But I don't know how to measure this year for Brady. I'm anxious to get to the end of this season so we can know what it is. To see what will happen in the next seven weeks."

"Have you ever met Brady?"

"No. Brady's people didn't communicate with me for this recent book or the others. I will say that the Patriots have been extraordinarily cooperative for other projects, but when I told Stacey James I was working on this most recent book about Brady being the best ever, he said 'Okay, no thanks.' That was it. They weren't arranging interviews with anyone. You can't cooperate with a book saying you're the best ever."

"What would you ask if you could meet Brady in person?"

"If I thought he would really answer? On a small level, I'd like to hear the true story about the pizza and Mr. Kraft."

Supposedly the year he was drafted in the sixth round, young Tom Brady was walking down a hallway at training camp, holding a pizza. At the time he was the fourth-string quarterback, just trying to make it on the roster, because professional football teams almost never keep four quarterbacks in a given season. Young Brady saw the Patriots' owner, Robert Kraft, and walked over to him.

The story goes that Brady introduced himself and declared: "Drafting me was the best decision this franchise ever made."

"I've heard so many different versions," Sean said. "Bob Kraft himself tells so many different versions of that story. At every speaking engagement. I know the reality has long since left that tale, so I'd like to know what really happened. If he really came in with that attitude."

So Tom. Did you actually say that to Robert Kraft? If so, you were right, of course. But what would you have thought this past preseason if some strapping youth walked up to the owner and said the same?

"I also would like to know," Sean said, "how much—and it's too big of a question to ask, but it's along the same lines: what is the reality and what is the myth?—how much of that in-first, out-last Brady thing is true? That working harder than anyone else. I mean, I know he's not Peyton Manning, he didn't come in anointed, chosen as the first player in the entire draft. [As too did Cam Newton.] Brady had to prove himself. He's had to earn everything. But no matter what you do, right, at some point the legend grows bigger than the man. And we might never get to that. Because after he leaves the game, Tom might not be able to help believing his own legend, embracing his own legend, believing the stories told about him. He might go into television, too. Like so many of these other guys, he might get out of the game and realize that he's addicted to being famous. He'd have offers from the networks in an hour if he wanted them."

"Do you have a prediction for the rest of the season? In September you predicted the Pats would beat the Broncos in the AFC Championship and then beat the Packers to win it all."

"I was looking at the rest of the schedule this morning. I think they're a twelve-and-four team. At worst eleven-and-five. I think it's going to shake out that the Pats play Indianapolis at home. And then they're at Kansas City or Denver. But I'm thinking way too far ahead."

"Do you have the faith—that they'll win it all this year?"

"I'm not sure through all I've written about the Patriots that I've ever got the Patriots faith. I'm a fan of the game. I mean, I hate the business—its homophobia, the violence, the advertising to children—but I do love the game. And I do think he"—Sean pointed to the photograph of Brady on the cover of my copy of his book—"is one of the good guys. One of the role models. Yeah, I suspect that they will beat the Panthers tonight. And publicly, I think the Patriots will beat the Broncos next, too. But we might meet them again in the playoffs — and it's hard to beat a good team twice in a season."

Just before leaving the interview, I asked Sean about what he feels like he has learned, that most average fans don't get.

"You think you know how brutal this game is. But you don't really know how much of a toll it takes on these guys' bodies over the course of a season, over the course of a career. I've spent time with guys like Joe Andruzzi. These guys are almost always playing hurt, and I don't mean with some bruises. By the time they get to the end of the season they are playing with some really meaningful injuries. That they somehow manage to overcome. Maybe it's because of the paycheck. I suspect it has a lot to do with who they are as competitors. I am sure that it's really unhealthy. They're raised to be these people. They don't know how to do anything else. You meet people like Steve Grogan, who in a lot of ways can barely walk now. Steve Grogan is a quiet person, and won't show you this, but I think that he, as much as anyone else, enjoys the legend of himself and is happy to have built that legend as the warrior quarterback that played through injuries. But I suspect that if he knew what the long-term costs of building that legend were, when he was doing it, he might have made some different choices. Which I suspect is true for anyone who has had a long career in this game."

"What about Brady?"

"Oh, I think everybody's the same. I think if you've played the number of years he's played in the league, you're going to have long-term physical problems. Serious physical problems. You don't get your knee rebuilt and then go out and play on it and expect to be walking comfortably when you're fifty, sixty years old."

Sean gave me the name of the person who is in charge of community and alumni relations for the Patriots, and he offered whatever other support he could. I rushed home before coming back over here to Pier 27 to watch the game. The van hummed to UMass and back without a single stall, I might add.

We're into the fourth quarter now against the Panthers. New England drove to score a touchdown to open the second half. It was the first time this season they've started a second half strong. Brady zinged it to Gronk on a little slant, and our monster tight end muscled in four more yards, dragging three defenders into the end zone. It's been a quarterback duel since. Neither Newton or Brady threw a single incompletion in the third quarter. It looked like the Patriots were going to run away with the game, especially after Brady hit Kenbrell Thompkins with a long ball across the middle, after which Thompkins spun and duked and nearly made it into the end zone. But Cam Newton, a full dozen years younger than Brady, kept answering back by converting huge third downs both through the air and with his legs. Talib is injured now again, too, so the Patriots don't have three of their starting cornerbacks.

"Are these injuries too much for even the great Bill Belichick?" asked the announcer. Ugh. Cam Newton just threw a touchdown pass with exactly one minute left in the game: 24–20, Carolina Panthers ahead.

It's coming down to one final drive again. A Pats fan I don't recognize leans over to me from another table and says: "I'm not even nervous. My nerves are so shot from the last games. I'm numb already from this season."

The broadcast shows footage of the comeback against the Saints a few weeks ago — that last-second iceman toss to Kenbrell Thompkins.

Brady is now driving them down the field with completions to Gronk — on a fourth and ten — and then to Amendola. Now a helpful pass interference call. Now Brady's almost picked off. Now they're at the seventeen-yard line with three seconds left in the game. Brady steps up in the pocket away from pressure, looks into the end zone, throws off his back foot and down into the middle. To Gronk. The pass is intercepted.

But wait, a flag! A flag is down.

"Hang on!" says the announcer. "They interfered with Gronkowski."

"No chance," says Mr. Little, pretending he's bored.

The replay shows Carolina star linebacker Luke Kuechly practically tackling Gronk before Brady released the ball. The referee gets on the mike and says: "No foul on the play. The game is over." The fans in Charlotte erupt.

"Told you," Mr. Little says.

The announcers discuss whether it was because Gronk was too far away, meaning that he could never have caught the ball. The camera catches Brady shouting at the referees walking down an alley toward the locker room. Backup quarterback Ryan Mallett, like a terrier, shouts at the refs, too.

The game is over. The Patriots are 7–3.

NOVEMBER 19 / 2:40 P.M.
MYSTIC, CONNECTICUT

I went for a good run this afternoon. I think this is the first time this fall that I've actually felt really good out there, actually enjoying myself as I bounded down the steps behind the Art Association, strode past the old clapboard houses of "Captains Row" beside the river, and even was almost not in horrible pain when going up the stretch of three hills toward the end of my route up past the old stone library. The cold air felt good in my lungs. I felt strong. I've been timing myself, but I still can't seem to break my twenty-minute barrier. I think it's in reach, though.

"I just need to execute better," I tell the reporters at my presser. "This route is a tough road, very good, very experienced. But I think if I execute, start fast, I can beat the time. Just thinking about the next run, that's it."

I nod toward Peter King of *Sports Illustrated*. He says: "You seem to be doing very well with your back and rib, after that tough car-seat installation injury. Are you going to be able to keep running this aggressively?"

I laugh. "Never felt better. Feels great. Just day to day now, and in the end it's the doctor's decision."

I smile with a slight wave as I step off the podium: "Thanks, guys."

NOVEMBER 20 / 10:15 P.M.
MYSTIC, CONNECTICUT

The Denver Broncos are next. The Broncos pressman has not replied to me about an interview with Wes Welker. But I just had this correspondence with Pressman James, the hardest-working man in the NFL.

I wrote at 9:41 p.m.

> Dear Stacey:
>
> Once again, thank you so much for the press conference access. I've sent Jonathan Kraft a follow-up paper letter requesting an interview, and I'll soon draft one to Tom in the hopes he'll reconsider after the season is over. I'll send that to him via Patriot Place, if that's okay.
>
> May I make three more requests? Again, this project will not extend beyond this season. I promise you won't hear from me again.
>
> 1. I'm coming to the Broncos game Sunday night. Is there any chance I could watch the postgame press conference? Again, I won't say a word, won't raise my hand, etc.
> 2. Might I have a short interview with Kenbrell Thompkins before the end of the season?

3. Could I come to visit you, to speak with you for twenty minutes, on what it is like to do your job, to have to deal with hundreds of people like me each year, managing the celebrity aspect of your players? I'd be honored to do this after the season, too — when things slow down for you presumably.

Thank you so much for considering this. I know this is a massive week.

Pressman James responded fourteen minutes later, at 9:55 p.m.:

Jonathan Kraft has respectfully declined.

I can't give you access to the press conference, but you can watch it (and each of his other press conferences) online at patriots.com.

We can probably arrange an interview with Kenbrell. Let me know how long you think you would need with him. We can probably do that in a couple weeks.

As for meeting, I would be happy to do that after the season.

Thanks.

Well, okay. That had some positives. It will be great to talk to the rookie receiver about Brady.

NOVEMBER 24 / 6:15 P.M.
FOXBOROUGH, MASSACHUSETTS

Two hours before the Broncos game. I'm at the Olive Garden restaurant in the strip mall just outside Gillette Stadium. I'm slurping hot soup and hot coffee at the bar, two hours before the game. I'm sick with a fever, but I just couldn't miss this. I tried to get Hoss and Lenny to go with me, but they couldn't spare the time.

Thousands of people are out tailgating in the freezing cold tonight. It's twenty-two degrees Fahrenheit out there, but with frigid gusts right out of the Arctic it feels like it's below zero. Hard-core fans huddle around red-hot propane heaters and flaming barbecues, and they chatter in portable tents or drink beers as they stand around their trucks and wear fur hats. I parked the van in the middle of it all, paid forty dollars to be close to the stadium, but I simply do not have the energy tonight to go around interviewing people what they would ask Tom. The restaurant is standing room only with football fans, all of them talking about strategies to stay warm.

This week it's been talk of another Manning vs. Brady matchup, the constant comparisons of the two. They bill this as Manning-Brady XIV, using roman numerals like the Super Bowl, even though the two players actually never physically play against each other during a game. Manning is often suspect in cold weather, particularly after his neck injury. Brady goes down if a defensive lineman breathes on him, particularly after his knee injury. Manning always has the better

stats. Brady is usually the winner in the biggest of games. Manning will retire first. Brady will retire first. Manning looks like a thumb, but he is funny and can act. Brady is awkward, goofy, and cannot act, but he is not only married to a supermodel, he *is* a supermodel. And on and on.

The Broncos, favored tonight, are 9–1 and have been an offensive juggernaut. New England is 7–3, and has stumbled through each win. And, again, Denver is the only team in the entire league that has a winning record against the Belichick-Brady-led Patriots.

Meanwhile this past week, Brady's personal media people posted a little video of him thanking everyone for his Face-book page hitting two million fans. "Let's go win together," he says, sitting on a rock with some autumn leaves and trees in the background.

What time will I even get home? I have to lecture on *Moby-Dick* at 9:30 tomorrow morning. I've got my copy of the novel here at the restaurant bar with me, so I'll put this journal away and review a bit before heading over to the stadium. I'll reread how obsessed Ahab tries to meet up with the faceless white whale, how "he at last came to identify with him, not only all his bodily woes, but all his intellectual and spiritual exasperations."

NOVEMBER 25 / 3:45 P.M.
MYSTIC, CONNECTICUT

I got home last night about 3:30, Lisa did wake-up with Alice for me at 5:15, and I limped to campus by 9:20 and led a class on *Moby-Dick*. We talked about Ahab being sympathetic despite his madness. He's fifty-four years old, the father of a young child, and assessing his life as he tries desperately to meet up with this white whale, this king of beasts, this looming entity that has come to define everything he doesn't understand and cannot have.

I came right home afterward and collapsed for a nap. I feel awful, but it was all worth it to see that game, by far the best meeting yet of the two future Hall of Famers, and the only one that has gone to overtime. It was the coldest regular-season game in the history of Gillette Stadium. And that might just have been the toughest, most heroic second half of football that Tom Brady has ever played.

So I left the restaurant with my journal, recorder, and copy of *Moby-Dick*. I geared up with every layer I could fit on my body and waddled over to the gate to see the Patriots and Tom Brady for my first-ever home game. I actually didn't make it up to my seat to see the kickoff because it took so long to get through security, since everyone was so bundled up. I was in the middle of a big crowd of drunks, and as we inched forward with pressure from behind I felt like I was going to be suffocated. Headline: "Stampede at Gillette Stadium Weeds Out the Slow, Short, and Sick." I gave up some ground but was able to burrow my way over toward a barricade. Here people were getting angry at the security guards and then shouting at the first-class ticket holders who strolled directly into a warmed ticket gate just to our right, which had no line whatsoever and appeared more as if they were entering a five-star hotel.

By the time I got into the stands, the Patriots were down 7–0. My seat was literally, and I'm not exaggerating, in the worst row in the entire stadium. It was in the back corner all the way at the very top of the third level. The only plus was that the wall provided a bit of a lee from the really aggressive wind gusts. I had wanted to see if the crowd gave Wes Welker a cheer when he came in, but I didn't get to my seat in time.

I had also missed the New England running back fumbling the football, and a Broncos linebacker returning it for sixty yards for the touchdown. As I settled in, the Patriots play on the field slid from bad to worse. It was if the ball were made of ice. The New England offense took the field again, and two plays later Brady dropped back to throw and got mugged from behind, then absolutely crushed from the front. He fumbled, and the Broncos' big, fat defensive lineman whom they call Pot Roast picked up the ball and rumbled another dozen yards, setting up a second touchdown for the Broncos. On the next possession a second Patriots running back broke a big run. He legged it almost up to midfield but then got thunked. And fumbled. Three minutes left in the first quarter, and it was 17-0 Denver.

In my section and throughout the crowd, fans began to boo. No one talked to each other. The stadium announcer's upbeat tone about the locations of various concessions sounded mocking.

The second quarter was almost as bad for the Patriots. Brady and Edelman each fumbled, but at least recovered their own balls. The Patriots tried a faster pace, going with a no-huddle offense. They tried to run. They tried deep balls. Nothing worked. Punts and more punts. Meanwhile the Broncos running backs and offensive line blew right through the Patriots defense whenever they had the ball. Welker didn't do much, but Manning barely had to throw. By halftime it was 24-0.

Speaking through his scarf, some guy in front of me explained to us "nosebleeders" that Tom Brady had never been down by this much at halftime in his entire career. Belichick hadn't either — even when he was head coach with the Cleveland Browns. A couple in their fifties to my right mentioned the *almost* comeback last year against San Francisco, also at Gillette Stadium. I watched that game over at Lenny and Elke's house. They went to bed, but I stayed up, and the Patriots came back after being down 31-3. In the end, though, we lost.

"I don't care about the Niners game last year," the husband said as the players jogged into the locker room. "Let's go, honey. This is a disaster. Let's just get this over with and don't let anybody else get hurt. Before I lose my toes to frostbite, let's just start driving to Houston to watch next week's game against the Texans. Where it's warm for Christsakes and we've got a chance of winning."

I walked down to the concession area to try to get out of the wind. Thousands of people left the stadium, streaming into the parking lots like frozen, bundled immigrants fleeing a shipwreck. I thought about leaving, too, because I felt sluggish and my ears and nose remained crammed with frozen snot. Instead I got the tallest mug of hot chocolate they served, and I bought some coffee to pour in the mug when the chocolate went down. I swallowed two DayQuils.

One good thing about everyone leaving was that I got a far better seat at midfield, just at the edge of the upper deck. Easily half the seats in the stadium were empty. In the red first-class seats on the other side, there wasn't a single high roller out there. They either left or were enjoying their warm bar-style seating behind the glass. Not that I blamed them.

I hadn't shaved in two days, and with all my hats and blue-and-maize scarf and shirts and down vest and long underwear and ocean foul-weather jacket and lined overalls and wool socks I felt like a molded, fat, frozen old scarecrow — left outside to mold some more and disappear under the frost. I know the fans in Chicago and Green Bay endure this sort of thing all the time, but it hurt whenever my scarf came down, and my glasses, which kept fogging up, made icy, sticky contact with the bridge of my nose. I coveted the ski goggles and masks that several other fans wore. The two requisite shirtless young maniacs with their painted chests, who regularly appeared on the Jumbotron, made me feel still colder.

Then our New England Patriots came back out on the field a different team in the second half.

Tom, what did Belichick or you or anyone else say in that locker room at halftime?

Brady and his offense drove down on the first series and hit Edelman sprinting one-on-one in the back corner of the end zone with a perfectly touched ball, low and around the defender: 24–7, Broncos lead.

Both Brady and Manning wore black balaclavas, but, objectively, whenever they flashed Peyton's face up on the Jumbotron, he looked old: bags under his eyes, shiny cheeks, and little jowls. Brady by contrast was a comic book hero, like the Black Knight or Batman. Maybe it was his eye-black, which Brady wears across his cheekbones, regardless of light conditions, or maybe Brady looked so much more badass because instead of wearing his knit ski cap or helmet like Manning whenever he sat on the bench, Tom kept his helmet off, his balaclava on, and he wore one of those huge dark football player sideline coats, like a cape. Brady was not a man that was giving up.

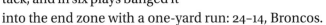

Peyton Manning, on the other hand, as the second half wore on—as the momentum began to shift so dramatically—had a nose-crunch stomachache disappointment face, an expression more common to his younger brother Eli.

The Broncos fumbled the football. The Patriots went to their hurry-up, no-huddle attack, and in six plays banged it into the end zone with a one-yard run: 24–14, Broncos.

When Manning got the ball back, he completed a couple of passes to Welker, to which the crowd couldn't seem to decide how to respond. (I saw one couple holding up big photographs of Welker and Brady on separate poster boards. Each ex-teammate was saying: "No, I miss YOU more!") Manning fumbled, recovered his own ball, but they needed to punt. The Patriots drove back sixty-five yards. Gronk posted up in the end zone like a power forward in basketball, and Tom flung it to him in the middle. After the catch Gronk spiked it so hard and so flatly it's a credit to the Wilson football factory in Ada, Ohio, that the ball didn't burst when bashed against the tundra. Brady ran up to Gronk, and the two of them shouted into each other's faces, all charged and pumped up like frat boys after guzzling funnels: 24–21, Broncos.

Brady paced the sidelines and energized his teammates. When rookie safety Logan Ryan intercepted Manning deep in Denver territory, all the fans who had stayed hollered themselves delirious. Brady ran on the field and three plays later connected with Julian Edelman on a short pass to the right. Edelman, the former Wes Welker understudy, spun out of one tackle and cut so sharply back toward the middle that two defenders flew past him. Edelman leaped high above a third defender, extending the ball into the air, and landed in the end zone: 28–24, Patriots now in the lead! Men waving Patriots flags ran around the field while the Patriots "End Zone Militia," dressed in Revolutionary War–era costumes, shot off their muskets into the air. Flares streamed from the roof of the stadium, and out of unseen speakers pumped some Bon Jovi guitar rock: "Whoa, whoa, whoa!" and "This is our house!"

By then I'd long forgotten about feeling sick or frozen. My new fellow fans, all separated by various empty seats, were an odd clump of people. A man in his fifties, at the bottom Plexiglas edge of our section, had exceptionally long arms and cheered silently. As the Patriots came back, he jogged in place, and with his ski gloves he jabbed, punched, and threw uppercuts, dancing to the blasting Bon Jovi. At first I thought he was eye-shut drunk, but as the game went on, I realized I was being unfair. He was in his own blissful, comeback world. He was a prizefighter in the late rounds. Two younger couples sat behind and in front of me. One pair wore Broncos gear; the other wore Patriots gear. The couples huddled together under blankets and looked miserable and often looked at me like I was insane. (I realized later that aside from my odd collection of layered gear, I also had hot chocolate and snot all over my frozen face.) The two couples never stood up or cheered or did anything. I have no idea why they stayed. A father and teenage son were to my lower right. They appeared to be having fun, but they didn't cheer loudly. I could see, though, that the dad wasn't comfortable because behind me, dressed in all black, wearing a beard, was an especially crass and profane Patriots fan. After Manning and the Broncos answered another Patriots field goal to tie the game with a touchdown, 31–31, sending it into overtime, the man grew more and more vocal. After a pass interference call on the Patriots, he belched a stream of gutter invective about the referee with an intense sexual vulgarity, describing the "zebras" and their injustices against the Patriots. When a Broncos player lay hurt, he screeched with gay slurs about the player faking it. This was all hard on the father. I stepped a few rows down from the man to make it clear I wasn't associated.

I'm never taking Lisa or Alice to a football game.

I tried to be a good fan, to clap when injured players left the field and to shout only positive things. But, man, I was into it!

I don't think I realized how much adrenaline I had until it was all over. I shouted things like: "Here we go now, Tom-AY! Let's get it back, now! Tom-AY! Hey, now, Pats!" Whenever we needed some defensive noise, I rapidly thumped two of the empty fold-up seats in front of me. I could feel how the young couples were staring at me, and the dad sometimes cheered late, almost as if he felt like he should have more passion but didn't quite have it in him. For my part, I simply could not help it. I was having the time of my life.

The Patriots had won the coin toss, but Belichick made the surprising choice to kick off to the Broncos and give Manning the ball first, betting that since the overtime rules now required the Broncos to score a touchdown on the first drive in order to win outright, they would not be able to do so *into the wind*. If Denver got a field goal, then New England going with the wind would have an easier shot to answer. Craggly, mean old Belichick bet against Peyton Manning in the cold weather. He got it right.

Overtime began, and the Broncos and Patriots traded short drives and punts for the entire period. With about three minutes left, a tie seemed likely. The Patriots lined up to punt to Wes Welker. The Broncos coach had decided that Welker should return the punts in overtime, because their normal punt returner had fumbled earlier in the game. The crowd sang: "Weeelker! Weeelker!" Though the coach denies this reason, pundits often say that Belichick prefers left-footed punters because the bounce is often unexpected. And this time, at about 12:30 a.m., the punt was an especially high and long one. Welker decided to wave off the kick, to not catch the ball and let it hit the ground at his own thirteen-yard line, anticipating it would tumble back into the end zone for a touchback. But he made the call too late. His blocker could not get out of the way. It bounced into the Denver player's knee and right into the arms of Patriots own special teamer,

Nate Ebner, who engulfed the ball like the last prized morsel of chocolate Hanukkah gelt! Mazel tov, Mr. Ebner! Mazel tov!

Brady grinned ever so slightly, ho-hum, and put on his helmet.

A couple of plays and a few formalities later, the Patriots kicker Stephen Gostkowski jogged in and sent the football through the uprights, with extra follow-through for flare: 34–31, Patriots. I put both hands on my head and looked up to the football gods.

Rifle shots from the End Zone Militia. Sprinting flagmen. Jumping cheerleaders. Fireworks exploded from both ends. The stadium now played Bruce Springsteen's "Glory Days," and the Jumbotron watched Wes Welker stroll off the field, and then showed Julian Edelman highlights. By the numbers this was the greatest comeback in New England Patriots franchise history.

I skated down the long stairs and out of the stadium on such a frozen river of good feeling and goodwill, sliding along with the pride among the fans who had stayed. I can't count the number of people who made eye contact with me and said, "How about that?" or "We did it!" and "We believed, didn't we?" and so on. The van started right up. I turned the heat to eleven. I sat in bumper-to-bumper traffic for two hours, guzzling down the warm postgame radio revelry. Not bad for my first game at Gillette.

Tom! Shackleton! Thor! Latobius! Moby! Must you kick so much ass, so often?

NOVEMBER 26 / 9:00 P.M.
MYSTIC, CONNECTICUT

Haven't heard from Pressman James in a while. So I just sent him this:

Hi Stacey:

Congratulations on Sunday's game. (I'm just about thawed out!) Might a 20-min interview with Kenbrell Thompkins still be possible? At his convenience, of course, but perhaps Monday or Wednesday afternoon Dec. 2, 4, 9, or 11?

And any possibility of press box access for the Cleveland or Buffalo games, the last two home games of the season?

Thanks so much,

Rich

NOVEMBER 30 / 9:40 A.M.
EN ROUTE FROM PHILADELPHIA
BACK TO MYSTIC, CONNECTICUT

On the train the Saturday morning after Thanksgiving. It was hard to find two seats, but I went down the aisle and said, "Mother and daughter looking to sit together, mother and daughter," and a nice young woman moved and let Alice and Lisa get the two seats. I'm just across the aisle. We thought we'd try the train instead of the van this Thanksgiving. About the only possible good thing with not having Ruby. My dad pushed the Volvo again this weekend, but I hemmed and hawed. When we drove their station wagon to go food shopping for my mom, Lisa said: "You look so handsome in the Volvo! Rugged and sexy at the wheel there." I'm not falling for it.

We had a really good weekend. Alice loves her grandparents and cousins. Lisa played tennis with my dad. I ran a loop from the house to my old elementary school, then to my middle school and back, which isn't very far. But when I was little it felt like thirty miles.

My uncle Frank, my dad, and I went to breakfast one

morning. Frank took out a pen and began to make cryptic notes and lines on a napkin, as if diagramming a play, planning my meeting with Tom. He drilled me with questions as to how it has been going so far. We drank our coffee and ate our lox and bagels, and even in my forties, it felt special to be at a diner with my dad and his younger brother—me still a kid among adults.

I asked Uncle Frank what *he* would ask Tom Brady.

He said, "Do I embarrass you?"

Thanksgiving night, after throwing the ball around on the front lawn, after watching a couple of NFL games with cousins and uncles, after all the other relatives left, and all the kids had their baths together and finally fell asleep, my dad and Uncle Frank stayed up and chatted—or I should say shouted at each other, because they're each a little hard of hearing. They talked as usual about sports: about the old Brooklyn Dodgers, about the old New York Football Giants, about the old great Jewish football players, about the old Jewish prizefighters—men named "Lefty" Lew Tendler and Louis "Kid" Kaplan. My dad and Uncle Frank kept several of us awake. I loved it.

Last night, Dumptruck picked me up in his truck, and we went to our twenty-fifth high school reunion. (Our wives both preferred to stay home.) I had a much better time than I expected, partly I think because nobody recognized me. I had been an extraordinarily, almost clinically late bloomer. When I graduated high school I weighed, honestly, only about one hundred pounds. I didn't really hit puberty until my freshman year in college.

So at the reunion, few could place me. They looked at the yearbook photograph, which the organizers had printed out for each of us to wear on our chests. The yearbook quotation I chose when I was seventeen was by Ralph Waldo Emerson. I'm surprised I picked this, as it was so obviously directed at my height, but the words mean so much more to me now, a lesson to my forty-three-year-old self: "There is a time in every man's education when he arrives at the conviction that envy is ignorance; that imitation is suicide; that he must take himself for better, for worse, as his portion; that though the wide universe is full of good, no kernel of nourishing corn can come to him but through his toil bestowed on that plot of ground which is given to him to till." Backyard boats, baby.

The reunion had all the stereotypes. Many dressed to the nines in order to impress. Some on second or third marriages. A guy who had been an all-state athlete back then is now overweight and balding and had far too much to drink. He came running up to me pretending he had a lacrosse stick in his hand and I was a goalie. Another guy pinned me in a corner for a while and told me how the current football players at my high school are soft, because they are now second- and third-generation white-collar kids. They don't play both sides of the ball, for example. He had been an offensive and defensive lineman. He recounted various games, forgetting that I never played high school football with him. People discussed old grudges and gossiped about those who weren't there. I saw a few long-lost classmates, and we shared the classic "I love you, man" and "We'll always be friends, even though we don't see each other often." I did mean it, though, and I hope they did, too.

I had been dreadfully afraid of the reunion small talk, so I brought a photograph of Lisa and Alice, and I wore my middle-school football jacket, from the seventh grade. The jacket had once meant a great deal to me. I found it up in my parents' attic yesterday afternoon. I could get it on, but it stretched tightly over my shoulders and barely buttoned across my chest. It was a fun and easier place to start the conversations.

Growing up I relentlessly played and practiced lacrosse,

since it was my primary point of self-esteem as an undersize teenage boy. But the pinnacle of any success I had in organized sports was actually in football. The moment I got that jacket.

My middle school had three football teams: the 105-pound and under "A" team, the 105-pound and under "B" team, and the "JV" team, which was for the boys that weighed *over* 105 pounds. In the seventh grade I tried out and was placed on 105-B. Dumptruck's mom would not let him play, but mine did reluctantly, despite her concerns about my inevitable paralysis, perhaps because she understood I'd never be able to play in high school. I weighed then, without exaggeration, about seventy pounds. Though occasionally I ran the ball on offense, I mostly played defense as an outside linebacker. Linebackers are meant to be good tacklers but also quick and agile to be able to stop the pass — although on the 105-B team there wasn't much intentional throwing of the ball in the air. I had played a lot of playground football and knocked around

with three older brothers, so I had a certain fearlessness about tackling, despite my size. The only helmet that I could find that fit comfortably, when they brought us into the big, gloomy equipment room, was designed for kickers: with one bar across the face. So I looked something like this:

At the start of the season we also chose the pads from wheeled canvas bins and learned how to slide the protective gear into the special pants. We chose and laced up our shoulder pads, and pulled down our socks to show our shins. I felt like a superhero when I walked out of that locker room. I remember the smell of that gray cell, the maroon lockers, the pine disinfectant lathered over the nostril assault of stale, grassy, teenage body odor. And the eye-black. Passing around that tube from player to player before the game. Looking in the mirror on the way out of the locker room. I know why Brady wears it every single game, whether he needs it or not. It's war paint. We'd punch each other's shoulder pads before a game. "Explode to the ball! Gooo Knights!"

The Bala Cynwyd Middle School 105-B Knights went undefeated that season. Ten wins, zero losses. This was almost entirely because we had Danny Rubin, a small, blond-haired kid who could accelerate so quickly through a tiny hole in the dusty scrum at the line of scrimmage that he scored at least two eighty-yard touchdowns every game. (He wasn't there last night, but someone said he went into his family's real estate business.)

At the reunion, I was amazed at some of the things old classmates remembered from high school and middle school. Lisa can rattle off the name of every teacher she's ever had. I can recall very little from my time in school. Except feeling out of place. But I do remember football. I recall being on that field, which looked so tiny when I jogged over there a couple of days ago. And I recall so vividly our pizza party the week after that final win of the 105-B football season in the seventh grade. We ate in one of the classrooms. Coach Wallace and Coach Booth sat at the head of the room. They presented us all with white faux satin jackets with our school name on the back, with the words "105-B Football" and "Undefeated" arched around an illustration of a ball. We were each handed gold pins to put on our jackets. Then Coach Wallace announced that I won the "Defensive MVP" Award. He gave me a certificate and a letter patch. His big hand shook mine roughly.

I was shocked. Elated. It was my first publicly recognized success in anything.

I strode home from school. Eight blocks. With my winter coat garishly unzipped, I marched on that autumn day under the spotty-bark sycamores, the red maples, crunching and kicking leaves on the sidewalk and holding that jacket, still inside the plastic bag. I held the award letters in my right hand, looking at them again and again. I hoped my mom could sew them on the jacket that night so I could wear it in school the next morning. I grinned and said aloud: "Yes, sir. Now things are going to change."

DECEMBER 1 / 1:40 P.M.
MYSTIC, CONNECTICUT

At the Pier 27 Lounge. The Patriots are visiting the Houston Texans, who have been a surprise doormat this season. Yet Houston is ahead of New England right now, thanks in part to a Brady interception. The Texans coach, Gary Kubiak, is back on the sidelines, after collapsing on the field several weeks ago. He had a minor stroke on his way into the locker room at halftime against the Colts.

I'm having a beer this afternoon because there's no MFL today. Lenny couldn't get anyone to commit—injuries, family obligations, work trips, and so on. I went for a jog this morning instead and went about a mile or so farther than my usual route.

Halftime. You know it's the holiday season because the commercials are no longer just beer, cars, and Viagra, but now also jewelry and gifts, with images of young men proposing and older men draping necklaces around their wives' necks.

New England is down 17–7. We look shaky. Brady took a brutal sack, a forearm to the head that earned Houston a roughing-the-passer penalty. Tom was slow peeling himself back up. The Texans run game plowed over the Patriots in the first half.

After Houston's second running touchdown, Gangly John sang "Deep in the Heart of Texas."

A bartender, wearing a pink Patriots number-twelve jersey, replied: "What were you singing last week, Mr. Broncos?" This got a big laugh across the joint.

. Third quarter and the Patriots, just like against the Broncos, look like a different team out of the locker room, having made whatever strategic or attitude adjustments. Tom is marching the team down the field with pass after pass. The only problem is that the Texans, even with their scrub quarterback, are answering right back. To start the fourth quarter, the Patriots are down 24–21.

Whoa — the man with the Patriots El Camino just came in the bar! And he's wearing a red Tom Brady jersey! As I observe him move around the place, he seems to be disliked here at Pier 27. Dolphins Guy, who is at his usual stool turned out from the bar, is having a hard time seeing around the man to watch his game, but he doesn't say a word to him. The kind woman who once placed a napkin by my plate seems the only one who responds in any way to the man with the El Camino. She does so with a guarded tone. He stands and watches the Patriots. Then he leaves to go get his pizza and drive off. I feel a little crestfallen. I had hoped to connect with this Patriots super-fan, to watch the game with him. To have everyone cheer when he came in. To see how he'd rally all the Pats faithful in the bar. Instead, there is an odd sort of unspoken relief among the assembled when he leaves.

DECEMBER 2 / 8:30 A.M.
MYSTIC, CONNECTICUT

I just mailed a paper letter to Tom, through Pressman James. It began this way:

Dear Tom (if I may):

Congratulations on Sunday's win in Houston, another fourth-quarter comeback. Stacey has told me he has already mentioned my project, but at the risk of being a pain, I'm writing again. . . .

DECEMBER 3 / 9:45 P.M.
MYSTIC, CONNECTICUT

Spoke today on the phone with Mike Reiss, a Patriots reporter for fifteen years, now working for ESPN Boston. I first saw him on the first day of training camp, interviewed on the radio show by two other Mikes. At the beginning of the season, he predicted the Patriots would go 12–4 but lose in the Super Bowl to the 49ers. He said he's sticking with that pick.

"I don't know how it's all going to end with Brady," Mike told me. "Either for this season or the rest of his career. All I know is that he is one guy who you just do not bet against. I would not bet against Tom Brady with anything."

"Do you have advice for someone trying to meet a superstar like Brady?" I asked. "Are there certain things that new sports journalists should *not* do?"

"Treat them just like you would treat anyone else. I think that's the biggest thing. Don't raise them up on a pedestal. Because they put their pants on the same way we do. I think they'll respond better to that. *Hey, this person looks at me like a peer, like an equal.* Versus treating them as an admiring, sort of like—you know? Which is really the way we should treat anyone, right? Even the president. We're all sort of the same. It's about who we are as people."

Tom, I read that after winning your three Super Bowls, you played golf with President Clinton and President Bush the Elder. What was that like? Since "The Photograph," have you stood in awe of anyone? Is there anyone who is on a pedestal to you?

DECEMBER 4 / 8:35 P.M.
MYSTIC, CONNECTICUT

In the news: two part-time security guards in Houston got fired for asking to take a photograph with Tom Brady after the Texans game. Brady seemed happy to pose with them—he's in a tailored tan suit, crisp white shirt, crisp white hand-kerchief in the breast pocket, and a dark violet tie—but this snapshot was apparently strictly against the stadium security policy. The incident made national news.

I went to the eye doctor this morning. She became almost girlish when I told her that I was planning to meet Tom Brady.

I had made the appointment because I'm starting to have difficulty reading fine print, such as the directions for Alice's board games. I find I need to take my glasses off to read things. I have to bring the words up close. I actually don't mind this part of getting old. I feel oddly distinguished when I have to take my glasses off to read. But I also wanted to ask the eye doctor about contacts. Lisa always says I look better without my glasses. I used to wear contacts, but then got too lazy.

"So what would you ask Tom Brady?" I asked the eye doctor.

"Does he wear contacts?"

"I don't know. I've seen him wear glasses in a couple photo shoots, but I think that was a fashion look. A Clark Kent sort of thing."

"That's what I want to know. Does he wear contacts. And what kind exactly? Rigid gas permeable?"

"Seriously? That's it? C'mon. Anything else?"

"No, really," she said. "I would really like to know that!"

DECEMBER 5 / 2:15 P.M.
MYSTIC, CONNECTICUT

Picked up Alice at preschool. She's napping now in her bed. After she fell asleep in the car, I turned on talk radio, and even though Peyton Manning seems the clear favorite, there are those making the argument that Brady should be this year's MVP for all that he's done with so little. But most experts think that it's unlikely the Patriots will be able to make a deep run in the playoffs.

Got a letter in today's mail from Uncle Frank, who typed, *with a typewriter*, some "sane and insane questions for the TB interview."

Here they are exactly:

1 Do you find my project ridiculous? Intrusive? Idiotic?
2 Do you know there are thousands of young men who look up to you as some kind of beacon of hope in their paralyzed lives?
3 What do you eat? Are you diet conscious?
4 Do you find it peculiar that in surveys—in spite of your Fat Cat lifestyle—you are considered a "man of the people"?
5 Do you look upon yourself, on the football field, as an artist? A technician?
6 As a kid—was there an athlete you idolized?
7 Is your extreme coolness on the field something natural—or constructed?
8 Would you redesign the field uniforms of the NFL if it was in your power?
9 What kind of books do you read?
10 In your leisure time, do you ever think about games and players from the beginning of your career?

11 Do you agree with the theory that pro football is so popular because it is the only sport that reflects the repressed communal violence of the human species?

12 Do you still believe in the God you worshipped as a child?

13 Are you a moviegoer?

14 Does it disturb you that everything about your life is so beautiful?

15 Was there any discussion about searching me for weapons prior to entering the interview room? As a kind of protection against a John Lennon type of event?

16 Are you musical?

17 Did you ever think about the fact that you came from California and you brought the "laid back" look into gridiron prominence?

18 Did you think that the recent comeback against the Broncos was so astonishing it had to signify that it was the apogee of your career — and you finally have started on the end game?

19 Are you at all interested in the social lives of animals or of primitive tribes?

Uncle Frank had gone back in with pencil to correct a few typos.

"Keep up the impressively lunatic project," he signed off. "Get it done. Meet that man."

DECEMBER 8 / 9:40 P.M.
MYSTIC, CONNECTICUT

Alice and Lisa asleep. No Ruby to pet.

I went to the Pier 27 Lounge this afternoon to watch the Cleveland Browns play the Pats at Gillette Stadium. I had a nice conversation with Loud Brady Lady and her husband, who told me they had made the trip to Charlotte for the Carolina game.

"What are you thinking about today?" I said.

"Oh, I always think they're going to win!" Loud Brady Lady said.

The games are starting to get critical for teams to either make the playoffs or establish seeding. Since the Patriots beat the Broncos, it's possible for them to get both a first-round bye and home-field advantage all the way through.

It's a blizzard in Pittsburgh for the Steelers hosting the Dolphins. Both teams have an outside shot at the playoffs, so Steelers Alley is loud and proud, while Dolphins Guy watches pensively. Despite the Steel Curtain opposite the serving area, I anticipated the halftime pizza and ribs and was able to slide in behind a block from Nick Name to nab both a plate and two slices before Gangly John even came in to box out with his gangly elbows.

In the third quarter Rob Gronkowski got walloped low by a safety in the open field after he caught one of his classic long seam patterns from Brady. Gronk lay on his side and meekly smacked the turf. The doctors drove him off the field on a golf cart, likely with a season-ending ACL injury. Mr. Little had a conniption.

The game was a defensive battle for three quarters. A couple of times I spied Loud Brady Lady on her iPad ordering Patriots gear for Christmas gifts. With Thompkins and Dobson now both injured, Brady was trying to get it going with yet another no-name rookie receiver.

Then late in the fourth quarter it got ridiculous, and the Patriots conspiracy theorists got more fodder. Brady now has five comebacks in the fourth quarter this year. They just get more and more improbable. With 2:39 left in the game, the Patriots were down 26–14.

"Can Tom Brady work magic again?" said one announcer.

"He'd have to do it more than once," quipped the other.

With no Gronk or Thompkins or Dobson, Brady tossed passes to Edelman, Amendola, and his running back Shane Vereen. Brady became the first quarterback all season to throw for over three hundred yards against Cleveland, one of the best defenses in the league. The Patriots quarterback drove the team down to the Browns three-yard line, then fired the football to the back of the end zone to Julian Edelman, who in the air took a brutal forearm to the head yet somehow still held on to the ball, like a road-kill squirrel still clutching a nut: 26–21, Browns. At this point the Patriots had only one minute left, and they had used up all their time-outs. They still needed another touchdown.

Every person in the stadium knew they were going for an onside kick.

"We haven't had a successful onside kick," announced Mr. Little, "since the New Year's Day playoff game almost twenty years ago. Which you'll all remember was against the Browns. When Bill Belichick was *their* coach. No way lightning's striking twice. This game's over, fellas. As is the season now, without Gronk."

But then they did get it! Stephen Gostkowski somehow

converted the kick right up the middle, almost recovering it himself. And their field position was even better because of the unnecessary roughness call on the guy who flattened Edelman.

"You just never walk out of this stadium unless there are double zeros on the clock," said the TV announcer.

Brady jogged in and went for the kill, throwing it deep into the end zone. Josh Boyce, the Patriots' third-string rookie receiver, drew a fairly suspect pass interference call, about which the home crowd didn't complain. On the very next play Tom rolled out to his right and slung it in stride toward Amendola, who sliced a little out pattern off an Edelman rub route. Amendola snagged it just within the goal line. Touchdown! Amendola threw the pigskin straight up in the air like a kid flinging skyward the first snowball of the year. Just ridiculous. New England wasn't able to convert for two, so it was a 27–26 Patriots lead.

As if all this wasn't enough, with thirty seconds left the Browns scratched back and got their kicker within range for a long but possible fifty-eight yarder.

"Miss it! Goddammit! Miss it!" shouted Loud Brady Lady.

"You all do not deserve this win," declared Gangly John.

The Browns kicker this year is Billy Cundiff, the same guy who missed a late, much shorter field goal in an AFC Championship game in Foxborough when he played for the Ravens.

"Billy Can-whiff!" shouted Nick Name.

With one second left, Cundiff missed. It was on line, but too short.

These wins just get crazier and crazier. This is New England's third late-game comeback in a row. If they can keep winning, if the goddess of fortune keeps shining down despite all these injuries, who is to stop them from the trophy and Brady's fourth ring? Why *not* New England this year?

DECEMBER 13 / 2:40 P.M.
MYSTIC, CONNECTICUT

At a school outside Boston, a few elementary school kids had been making fun of a boy named Danny who was born with a brain hemorrhage. Danny likes to wear a suit, tie, and fedora to school every day. He is the water boy for the town football team. So another kid, a fifth-grade quarterback—named Tommy—took it upon himself to defend Danny and organized the entire team to wear ties and fedoras one day at school to support their friend with special needs.

This morning I watched Danny, Danny's mom, and Tommy tell their story on *The Ellen DeGeneres Show*. After the guests explained to Ellen and the audience what happened, the host directed them to a screen on which Tom Brady appeared via satellite.

"Hi Danny and Tommy," Brady said. "I hope you're having fun in LA with my friend Ellen. I heard about your story, and I can't imagine how proud your parents must be. Danny, people still tease *me* about what I wear, but I never listen to them, so keep wearing what makes you feel best. And Tommy, I love your leadership and how you stood up for Danny, and I applaud the entire Bridgewater Badgers team for participating."

Tommy, the fifth-grade quarterback, is stunned by what he watches on the screen, and when Brady explains he has tickets to the final home game for them, his and Danny's mouths open wide at the same time. Danny begins to clap, and Tommy shakes his head and nods and smiles all at once.

DECEMBER 14 / 8:30 P.M.
MYSTIC, CONNECTICUT

I've printed out a letter to send to Tom Brady's agent in Los Angeles. I wrote: "Through Stacey, Tom has understandably declined an interview after the season is over, but I'm hoping you might be able to convince him otherwise."

DECEMBER 15 / 9:10 P.M.
MYSTIC, CONNECTICUT

"Looks like it's just the three of us."

"Because there's five inches of snow on the ground."

"Cool balaclava."

"Thanks!"

"Looks badass. Hey, where are your glasses? And what is that? A tube of antifungal cream?"

"No, Hoss, it's eye-black. Want some?"

"But it's completely cloudy."

"So?"

"All right, give me some."

"Me, too," Lenny said.

"I'll play steady QB."

"Better I'm steady QB. I've got my bad knees."

"But I've got this back thing."

"Do either of you know how painful a sports-groin injury actually is?"

DECEMBER 16 / 10:40 A.M.
MYSTIC, CONNECTICUT

We all just came back in from outside. Lisa did some cross-country skiing. Alice's first time ever sledding.

I heard back from Pressman James. He wrote to me at 6:22 this morning, the morning after an ugly New England loss in eighty-degree Miami. The game was yet another chance for a fourth-quarter comeback, but Brady was intercepted in the end zone on the last play. This season, the nail-biters have been nothing short of absurd.

Pressman James wrote to me: "Tom is still a decline, and I would suggest we target a veteran player rather than Kenbrell. In all likelihood, I would think the best opportunity would be to do something in the offseason."

I replied right away. In retrospect my response was far too long, explaining more about my project, how it wasn't to make money off Tom, how meeting Kenbrell really would be helpful, but any receiver would be great. I told him about how I've been reading David Halberstam's book on Bill Belichick (Halberstam spoke at my college graduation), and I asked Pressman James if there were any bones he could throw me before the close of the season and into the playoffs. Is that a common phrase, "to throw a bone"? He'll know what I mean, right?

DECEMBER 19 / 9:15 A.M.
MYSTIC, CONNECTICUT

Gisele posted an Instagram photograph of her being pampered by three separate stylists—one on her nails, one working on eye makeup, and another curling her hair. Gisele is wearing a thick white bathrobe as she openly breastfeeds her and Tom's infant daughter Vivian. Her caption: "What would I do without this beauty squad after the fifteen hours flying and only three hours sleep. #multitasking #gettingready."

Back in my house, Lisa and Alice staged an intervention, declaring that my Patriots hat is now "absolutely too manky" for wearing in public. I pleaded for leniency until after the playoffs, when (or if!) the Patriots lose. They acquiesced, but Alice is allowed to put it into the garbage immediately afterward. She said she's going to use the gardening gloves. #saveourmankycaps

DECEMBER 20 / 10:15 P.M.
MYSTIC, CONNECTICUT

The NFL continues to promote its "Together We Make Football" campaign. They're encouraging the public to click on the website to vote for their favorite finalists. The winners will get tickets to the Super Bowl and a slot in the league's feel-good documentary. One of the finalists is a woman named Heidi Gilbert, an animator who was having difficulty early in her career. Then she learned about Tom Brady, read about his draft analysis out of Michigan of being too slow, too skinny, and without enough arm strength to play in the NFL. She started to follow Brady and the Patriots, and in turn she began to get her groove back. Brady "helped me find the courage to be an artist again," she says in her video. Heidi was inspired by the quarterback's own comebacks, his fiery competitiveness, and his believe-in-yourself gestalt.

Headline: "Man Learns He's Even More of a Cliché Than Previously Thought." Click here for more. Or click here to send your old junker to "Mystic Backyard Boats."

I wrote to Heidi Gilbert.

DECEMBER 21 / 9:50 A.M.
MYSTIC, CONNECTICUT

I waited about forty minutes at the Department of Motor Vehicles to arrive at the front desk and to be turned away in less than sixty seconds by a droid-woman who explained that I could not register the Volvo because (a) my insurance is not effective until Monday (it is Saturday); (b) I have not passed emissions yet—this needs to be done *before* registration even if the car has passed recently in Pennsylvania; and (c) a spouse's driver's license number is insufficient—I need to have a photocopy of Lisa's card. I gave droid-woman

181

my idea of having a camera at the DMV that would randomly film people and display it on their screens, as they do with the Jumbotron at football games.

She said: "Next. Number forty-seven, please."

"What would you ask Tom Brady if you were able to get a real, non-Belichickean answer?"

"Number forty-seven, please."

So I drove the half-hour back home and then to the emissions inspection place. They were closed this morning, according to the note on the door, because of a family reunion. I went back home and then back out again to buy a replacement printer cartridge for our printer/scanner to copy Lisa's license. The store was out of the cartridge we need. I hate this Volvo.

Tom, when was the last time you went to the DMV?

DECEMBER 22 / 9:30 P.M.
MYSTIC, CONNECTICUT

The Baltimore Ravens won the Super Bowl last year after knocking off the Patriots handily in Foxborough in the AFC Championship. New England was far ahead at halftime, but, again, cornerback Aqib Talib went down, allowing Ravens quarterback Joe Flacco to air it out while his team's defense shut out Brady completely. This season, the Ravens started slow but are on a tear now. We played them this afternoon in Baltimore. No one picked us to win. Tom seems to always have a tough time against the Ravens.

No MFL game this afternoon because everyone has holiday obligations. Last week it was only Lenny and I playing with two teenagers that were hanging around. One of the teens said after I ran back a kickoff: "What are you, Julian Edelman?" Lenny and I had a good laugh at that. I'm afraid that the MFL is done for this year, for this season, fading out with a whimper.

So this afternoon instead of an MFL workout, I put on my Patriots hat and my cheap Tom Brady youth medium jersey that I bought for Halloween. I ran my route as hard as I could, going fast from the start, and really pounding on the last stretch, up the three hills to the old library from where you can look down on the river. I thought about the Patriots game, the team getting ready in the locker room. I pretended I was digging deep during the fourth quarter against the Ravens' intimidating pass-rushing linebackers. Sprinting on the final stretch, gasping for breath, I beat my previous record by a full minute and ten seconds.

The Patriots went on to embarrass the Ravens, who came out flat and stayed flat and got every wrong bounce and referee's suspect call. Even without Gronk, we avenged last year by handing the Ravens their largest home loss in the history of their team. It looks like the defending Super Bowl champs aren't even going to make the playoffs. Nick Name had a field day with their quarterback, Joe Flacco, who was playing with an injured knee and looked limp all game. Even Mr. Little broke a smile. Gangly John didn't care, though, because this afternoon, despite Wes Welker being out with a concussion, Peyton Manning beat Brady's single-season touchdown record. And there's still one more game to go to pile it on.

As the Patriots-Ravens game wound down and Steelers Alley began celebrating their own win that keeps them in playoff contention, a man in his forties, easily six foot seven, walked into Pier 27 dressed as an elf. He held a container of maple syrup and wore a Green Bay Packers jersey. Instinctively we all turned to Nick Name, who seemed the only one who could capitalize on a holiday vision this laden and bizarre and wonderful. But he was speechless. His fingers clenched. His lips parted. He knew it was his moment of glory. The ball was in the air. It dropped. Mr. Little went over and sat next to him and bought him a drink.

After the final whistle of the Patriots victory, I spotted Pressman Stacey James on the TV. He wore a long, dark coat and walked on the field beside Tom. I knew it was the pressman because last week, after much scrolling around on the Internet, I finally found a single photograph. And there he was tonight—oval face, short brown hair, pale eyebrows—gliding wordlessly beside Tom like a member of the Secret Service.

DECEMBER 29 / 2:40 P.M.
SAN FRANCISCO

I'm at the Buccaneer Bar, which is, despite the incongruous name, the top-rated New England Patriots sports bar in San Francisco. We're in California staying with family near Golden Gate Park. I got a late start from the house and was waiting a long time for the bus. It was taking a while to arrive, and when you're in a strange city on strange public transit, there's very little to trust. It was about forty minutes to game time. The Buccaneer Bar is in the Russian Hill district. So I figured, well, maybe I can make it by jogging there? I was wearing my running shoes, but I had on jeans, and had a bag with my journal, a book, and my audio recorder.

I waited five more minutes, then started running along Geary Boulevard. The bus soon belched past me with some of the people who had been at my stop, now looking smugly at me out the window. I tried to hustle to the next stop to get on, but I realized I was able to keep pace with the bus because of all the traffic, and maybe even make better time. I kept hoofing it up and down the hills, passing the bus, getting passed, and back and forth, until I was sopping with sweat. I kept checking the bus maps at the stops to check my location, looking at my watch. It didn't seem I was going to make it for kickoff, even though I was running as hard as I could. The hills were steep, my lower back cringed, and my arches began to hurt with so much slapping along the uneven pavement. Yet even when the bus passed me finally for certain, I kept running hard. I kept thinking of how I had helped the team pummel the Ravens.

I made it here to the Buccaneer Bar with two minutes to go, which even included one wrong turn on Polk Street — a hip area of coffee shops and sushi. I was sprinting full speed downhill when I finally found the bar. My jeans were half falling off, but I had a good feeling about this destination, having read online that every football Sunday it was standing room only with "ex-Pats" — New England–born fans living here in San Fran. And this was the last game of the regular season. Everyone had to be pumped up, too! A first-round playoff bye is at stake! So seconds before kickoff, I burst into the Buccaneer, shouting "Yeah, Pats! Here we go now!" I reached my hands up for high fives as I ran the gauntlet through the front door and along the length of the bar. "Go, Pats! Wahoo!"

Crickets. Although the bar was indeed nearly full, I met with surprised stares by the kindest of them and condescending looks of disgust by the less welcoming. The clinking of thin glasses. The clear voice of the announcers on TV. I received two soft high-fives from two men wearing Patriots jerseys who tapped my palm without looking, embarrassed.

Cowed, I found a stool at one corner. The bartender has since treated me with sympathy. This place is filled with 90 percent Patriots fans, but I've seen more active clientele in a research library. I guess I did enter as somewhat of a lunatic.

That was probably twice the distance I've run yet this fall, and certainly the longest I've sustained that speed. I kept thinking I was not going to make it. Certainly not that I could keep up that pace. Yet even after my mortifying entrance to the bar, I thought as the game began: *There's no way we can lose now.*

And this has proved true. It's now late in the fourth quarter, the crowd at the Buccaneer has warmed up, and people are now clapping and occasionally whispering positive comments. In contrast to the bright weather here in San Francisco, it's dark, pouring rain, and cold in Foxborough. Belichick wears two hoods. The Patriots uniforms are black, because they're soaked. Steam rises out of the players' silver helmets. Patriots running back LeGarrette Blount, at 250 pounds, has been an unstoppable force today, running for nearly two hundred yards, two touchdowns, and also two long kick returns, including one for over eighty yards. He has barreled and slid through puddles on the turf, juked defenders, and run right over others. As the clock winds down for a 34–20 win, Tom looks suspiciously from under his helmet.

This decisive victory against the Buffalo Bills bookends a 12–4 season and secures for Belichick and Brady the most division titles by any coach-quarterback tandem in NFL history. On another TV screen behind the bar, the Denver Broncos are decimating the Oakland Raiders in their stadium just across the Bay. Manning has broken Brady's single-season passing yardage record today, and his offense collectively topped the Patriots' 2007 season record for most points by any team in NFL history.

So I've sat at this bar drinking a beer all game, staying especially quiet. The sweat has dried on my back. I've stiffened up mightily. I'll be taking the bus back. My brother-in-law works in video-game production. He's got a gigantic flat-screen TV. He said he'd show me how to play Madden Football. Patriots vs. Broncos, of course.

JANUARY 1, 2014 / 10:44 A.M.
SAN MATEO, CALIFORNIA

The story goes that Tom Brady Sr. took his youngest of four kids to the San Francisco 49ers NFC Championship game at Candlestick Park to watch Joe Montana. (I, too, as it happens, am the youngest of four.) Tom Jr.—Tommy—was just four years old at the time, wearing a little Montana jersey, and he was, according to an ESPN writer, very upset most of the game because his father wouldn't buy him a foam #1 finger. But Tom Jr. still remembers what turned out to be one of the most famous football games in the history of the NFL. With less than a minute left in the NFC championship, Montana, after leading a drive from his own ten-yard line to the Dallas six, rolled out to his right as three Dallas Cowboys, taped up like mummies, ran savagely after him. Fading backward off his right foot, Montana sailed a spiral over their fingers —a ball that seemed flung out of the end zone to safety. His thin and rangy receiver, Dwight Clark, at six foot four, loped along the back line from the left and seemed to rise up in the air, plucking the pigskin at full extension like a country boy leaping up with two hands to nab a piece of fruit off a tall tree on his way home from school. Tom Sr. and Tommy had seats behind that end zone and saw the whole play. Young Tommy Brady heard that mad crowd roar. He saw Joe Montana's golden smile, the elation of that win, the cameras' flashes—the first of what would be a string of glory that would include four Super Bowl titles in four tries for Montana and the San Francisco 49ers.

There's a photograph out there of young Tommy Brady wearing his Montana shirt while tailgating with his family outside Candlestick Park. It looks much like this:

Growing up in San Mateo, California, about twenty minutes south of Candlestick, Tommy played baseball as a kid, playing catcher. He kept going with his dad to see Joe Montana and the Niners. In high school, Tom first began to play football along with baseball, getting the most time on the freshman team as an outside linebacker. He worked his way up to be the starting QB his junior and senior years.

He did well individually, but his teams were mediocre.

After Michigan, Tom Jr. and his family—season-ticket holders for some twenty-five years—hoped that he might try to play for the 49ers, to play in the wake of Joe Montana and Steve Young. San Francisco instead drafted another quarterback in the third round that year, far above Brady. The quarterback they drafted, out of Hofstra, turned out to be ill-equipped for the pressures of big-time professional football and never started a regular-season game in the NFL.

Right now, as I write, I'm sitting by a little stone press box at the Brady Family Stadium at Junipero Serra High School, the Jesuit all-boys school where Tom went in the early 1990s. It's clearly a California high school because the roofs are nearly flat and the vast swimming pool is outside. The stadium is modest but has a high locked fence around the turf.

It's New Year's Day, so there's not much happening on campus. For months I've been corresponding with multiple people to get an interview or tour of the school, but in the end I was unable to arrange any meetings, mostly because I could visit only during the holidays. When I got here this morning, New Year's Day, I did find a small group of students from the robotics club tinkering in a workshop opposite the field. I chatted with them for a while. Their instructor, who kindly walked me around the school, was proud to speak about Serra. "No distractions, and no bullshit here," he said.

He walked me into the locker room — where I saw a signed Tom Brady jersey in the coach's office — and we toured a part of the school. I looked into the classrooms, art rooms, and into a basketball practice in the gym. Brady was featured on an athletics Wall of Fame, but not more so than several others, in part because other famous pro athletes had once gone to this high school, too, notably the Pittsburgh Steelers wide receiver Lynn Swann and the baseball slugger Barry Bonds. I walked further along the linoleum hallways and found Tom in his 1995 class picture, on the top row of ovals, in alphabetical order. All the boys were dressed in tuxes. Tom looked then very much like an old high school friend of mine, an Irish Catholic kid named Patrick Daly, whom I saw at reunion this year.

On my way out I thanked the robotics instructor and the kids in the club. A senior among them, Isaac, was a perfect representative of Tom's alma mater. He loved it at Junipero Serra High School. He said he didn't feel like there is any conflict with jocks vs. academics at the school, among "the brotherhood," as he referred to the students, although he did point out that there aren't any pep rallies for anything but sports. Another kid commented how the football guys often stick their heads in to see what the robotics club is up to. How they're genuinely interested.

Isaac said school administrators invoke Tom Brady's name often when there is a discussion about alumni at Serra. "His name comes up a lot in classes, too. In my physics class, the teacher asked an extra-credit question: What grade did Tom Brady get in physics when he was here? And our English teacher used to coach Tom Brady in football. And teach him in his English class. He has all of Tom Brady's essays on a floppy disc. That's how they used to turn them in. Our teacher doesn't know how to read them anymore, though, off that kind of disc!"

As he spliced two wires together, another student in the club, named Will, added: "Our teachers talk about how Brady started off small, and then got really big. That's the simplest way to say it. Keep going, keep trying. You'll eventually succeed."

"What *did* Tom Brady get in physics?" I asked before I left.

"He got an A," Isaac said. "Both semesters. A's."

3

NOW THINGS
ARE GOING TO
CHANGE

JANUARY 2, 2014 / 5:15 P.M.
SAN FRANCISCO

Wrote this today to Stacey James: "Is there any chance you might be able to assist me with a ticket to the playoff game as a member of the press?"

In case he doesn't come through, I bought a nosebleed ticket to the playoff game online. I figure the price is going to go up once they know what team we are going to play. It depends who wins the wild-card games this Saturday.

JANUARY 7 / 9:20 A.M.
EN ROUTE FROM SAN FRANCISCO
TO PROVIDENCE

After ordering, I asked the flight attendant: "Could I ask you a non-beverage-related question?"

Lisa nudged me in the ribs.

"I believe you just did," he said.

"Ah, okay, good one," I said. "Can I ask you a second one?"

"You see what I just did? There's two!"

"I, yes, I did. Good. What would you ask Tom Brady?"

"I don't know. What *would* I ask Tom Brady?"

"No, no, it's not a lead to a joke. I'm a journalist and I'm planning on meeting him. I'm taking questions to him from The People."

"Hm. I'm not sure," he said. "I'll get back to you by the end of the flight."

"Must you do this everywhere?" Lisa laughed.

"I'm telling you, he's going to come back with something good. I can tell by now; I can tell who are the people that have thought carefully about Tommy."

Although I reminded him, the flight attendant never came back to me with anything besides another orange juice.

JANUARY 9 / 10:40 P.M.
MYSTIC, CONNECTICUT

It's going to be the Indianapolis Colts coming to Foxborough to play for the quarterfinals, aka the divisional round. We're favored by a touchdown, but the Colts are on a blaze of a winning streak and just came back from an absurd twenty-eight-point deficit to beat the Kansas City Chiefs. Meanwhile, Tom has been named to the Pro Bowl for the ninth time. Peyton Manning was voted the league MVP, with only one dissenting vote for Tom. "[Brady] carried that team," that single analyst said in an interview after the vote.

One sportswriter declared that Bill Belichick should be a candidate for Coach of the Year. He added: "The Patriots have lost the most important players on their defense, they've been decimated on offense, and yet . . . they're in the running to go to the Super Bowl."

JANUARY 11 / 7:15 P.M.
FOXBOROUGH, MASSACHUSETTS

What a mob scene! The van and I are sardined into a private parking lot about a half mile from the stadium. It's a torrential rain and dark as a pocket, but at least it's not nearly as cold as the last time I was here. As I drove along the main road to the stadium, I saw four cars pulled over for one reason or another. Then right in front of me, I watched a maroon sedan suddenly drive sharply into the opposing lane, making a sudden ill-timed decision about where he wanted to park. He got slow-motion crunched by a Jeep going in the other direction. Much yelling and cursing ensued. Perpendicular headlights in the rain, police sirens, orange flares, and flashing blue and red lights. I was happy to pull into this lot unscathed, although then a guy bumped me after I was parked.

He was embarrassed and apologetic. He had crumpled his front license plate into my van's trailer hitch. No harm done. "Go Pats!"

Tailgaters in this lot have rigged tents from car roof to car roof, under which they've set up barbecues, heaters, and large television sets. Sound of generators, raindrops on metal roofs, raindrops on tarps, and the sizzle of hot dogs and burgers. A few televisions are playing simultaneously the second half of this afternoon's other playoff game, in which the Seattle Seahawks are shoving the New Orleans Saints off the Super Bowl runway.

I just got back from jogging around all of the tailgating lots. I put on my Patriots number-twelve youth medium jersey, running shorts, and my manky Pat Patriot hat. I slid the audio recorder into a ziplock bag so I could interview as many people as I could before the game. It was a pretty tough crowd out there, I have to admit. I got heckled a few times about my

jersey, my pale legs, and the very act of jogging around in the rain. But I also got several cheers, too, as I ran from parking lot to parking lot. "Get going, Tom," said one guy. "You're late for warm-ups!"

Sitting in the van now and transcribing while I listen to all the tailgating revelry around me. There's a leak coming in around the gasket of the front windshield, but since I have rusted holes in the passenger floor, it's just dripping right back out. I can smell the shrimp the guys are grilling two cars over. It's pouring in Seattle, too, and I can hear on their TV that the Saints are trying to make a game of it. I'm covered in mud because the last, farthest of the tailgating fields are dirt lots.

I interviewed over sixty people, making about nineteen stops, at random, to tailgaters who looked serious or intriguing or inviting or who made fun of me. At sixteen of my nineteen stops, at least one person in each group wanted to ask Tom about his wife. These ranged from tame ribbings, such as "Can I have Gisele's number?" or "How does it feel to beat out her old boyfriend Leonardo DiCaprio?" to bawdy questions from both men and women who had been tailgating too long, had "lubed up," and wanted to ask about Gisele's performance in bed and various sex acts and other cringeworthy questions I can't write here.

The rest of the questions and advice and comments for Tom were a grab bag. Here are a few examples:

> Fan from the Boston area: "Does he think he's better than Peyton Manning? What does he really think of Peyton?"
>
> A man in his fifties, standing in a group of five men and one woman who had no tent or tarp or even proper raincoats, blasting grunge rock from their truck, drinking beers: "What is it like to be a god among men?"

Tall guy in his thirties: "I want it on record that I am still not buying UGGs, no matter how much I love the guy."

One young man tailgating with friends: "This game is just a formality on the way to the Super Bowl. And I do think Tom's going to know when to quit. It's not about the money for him. He just wants to be a Patriot for life. The Patriots are the only ones that took a chance on him in the sixth round. Got to stay loyal."

A downtrodden guy in his mid-fifties with a raspy voice: "Since returning from your injury, how come you've walked off the field nonchalantly at the end of every loss in the playoffs the last five years? It's like it just didn't matter to you." His wife: "Brady's excellent for the team. He's great. He's phenomenal. I'd ask him what is he going to do to make himself even better, to keep himself in the game for the next few years. But win or lose tonight, I'm proud of him."

One of four brothers tailgating in a distant, mud-pit of a parking lot: "How does he get across the moat at his house? Does he have some little boat?"

On my run back to the van, I invited myself into a gigantic enclosed tent with a television inside and an entire ping-pong table set up in there. Parked beside this tent was a vintage white Chevy van tricked out entirely with Patriots regalia. I had seen this on the road and had honked in celebration when I was driving up from Connecticut. His van had "Go Pats" painted all over it and Patriots stickers on both sides and a Patriots helmet glued to the roof. Yellow uprights were fixed on the back of the van, with a Nerf football glued in between. An American flag waved from astern. The man who owned it, in his early sixties, had a long white beard and told me it's only to bring to the stadium for tailgating.

The funniest response of this whole pregame jog, which I

hope is enough of a physical commitment to bring the Patriots luck, was from a pudgy guy with a Fu Manchu, making fun of me and my youth medium shirt. He said: "How does Brady feel about the fact that you're running around in his jersey?"

All right! The Pressman Stacey James never wrote back to me with a press pass, so I've got my Internet ticket in my pocket. Dry shoes and socks, check. Raincoat and rain pants, check. Keys, wallet, check. Here we go to the playoff game! Go Pats! Let's go Tom-AY!

JANUARY 12 / 3:45 P.M.
MYSTIC, CONNECTICUT

Got home last night around 2:30 in the morning, driving back in the rain listening to the postgame radio talk and all the people, including the hosts and experts, declaring that they are ordering their tickets for the Super Bowl.

Since I was by myself—Hoss almost came, but then had a family event—my plan was to find some unclaimed seat on the first level. I went over to the section overlooking the towering corridor where I had gone into the press conference about two months ago. This is where the Patriots come out onto the field before the game. I wanted to get a close look at Tom and the rest of our team as they sprinted out. The problem was that I didn't anticipate the blow-up tunnel helmet thing from which the team parades out before sprinting through fireworks and smoke. I had a great spot right along the rail, but then they wheeled out the blow-up thing and inflated it. I couldn't see anybody when they came out.

Tom, I see that the quarterbacks are the only ones who run out of there without their helmets on. Is that purely for television? Is it one person's job to carry your helmet?

I hung around that section for the entire first quarter and shuffled around as people arrived. I got a few annoyed looks, but most people knew what I was doing and didn't begrudge me, as far as I could tell. Our team wore their dark blue marine jerseys with silver pants, while the Colts were in all white with blue trim, wearing their white helmets with the blue horseshoe logo.

Andrew Luck, the young star quarterback of the Colts who also wears number twelve, threw an interception on the third play of the game, which was nearly run back by Patriots cornerback Alfonzo Dennard into the end zone, directly toward my section. I had the perfect view. Then LeGarrette Blount banged in the touchdown. It was 7–0 before I even got nodded out of my first seat. The End Zone Militia fired their muskets, the fireworks went off at the top of the stadium, the flag men ran around in circles, Pat Patriot mascot pumped his fists and skipped around, the cheerleaders shimmied their pom-poms, and the speakers cranked Bon Jovi's "This Is Our House."

The next time the Patriots got the ball, Tom and our offense drove all the way back down the field, toward me, throwing four completions in four tries, but mostly running the ball. Blount crashed it into the end zone again, and it was 14–0 Patriots. The stadium began to feel like a big happy festival. The people in my section began to shout slowly "Braaady! Braaady! Braaady!" and then added quickly at the end, like at a college game: "We want more!"

By the end of the first quarter there was nowhere left for me to stand in that lower section. As I had against Denver, I wore my offshore foul-weather jacket, the same coat I'd used when I sailed across the Atlantic. I hoped this would keep me dry and bring Tom some more good fortune. But my high-tech waterproof coat could not keep my e-ticket dry. The ink on the paper bled, and I could no longer read my seat number.

I didn't want to be a nosebleeder in the rain, anyway, so I stood to watch the second quarter under the eave of the second level, leaning on a rail beside the stairs. This is a popular spot among men over fifty, it seems. It had a certain appeal, as if we were watching the horse races in the 1940s or some other vision I'd seen in black and white movies. Out of the rain, we all put our elbows on the rail, watching in a line as we continued to hold the lead—but tenuously, as the Colts kept it close. We watched a long snap sail over our punter's head and tumble toward our own end zone. The rookie got pummeled as he tried to recover the ball and foolishly tried to throw it to one of his teammates. Fortunately, the Colts only got a safety out of it. It could've easily been a touchdown. But our punter was knocked out of the game, with a shoulder injury. Kicker Stephen Gostkowski did the punting from then on, and Tom held the snaps on extra points. We were up at halftime, on the back of three LeGarrette Blount touchdowns.

I tried to roll out my e-ticket on the top of a trash can, to go find my seat since the rain had eased, but it was still no use. I threw it out and walked up to the second level and found a good spot in the open in the same corner above the tall corridor, overlooking the end zone, with a good rail to lean on and no one behind me.

A tall security guard with dark dreadlocks came over to me. I expected him to move me along.

"Just go inside this red line, okay?" he said. "Put your *back* to the rail. That's a good spot, right?"

He was the kindest, most genuine person I'd met all day. I now stood behind a family of New England fans, a mom and dad with two tall brothers in their mid-twenties who held draft beers in plastic cups.

We received the ball after the half, but Tom and his offense went three and out. The Colts answered with a field goal. I began to get nervous. If you count the Colts' last playoff game, Andrew Luck had led the same number of fourth-quarter comebacks this year as Tom, and if his team got another touchdown tonight, they'd take the lead.

Tom answered by leading a drive that declared definitively the outcome of this playoff game—his eighteenth win in the playoffs, more than any other quarterback in history. More than Joe Montana. This drive punched our team's ticket for our third AFC Championship game in a row. And sent thousands of Patriots fans online to buy Super Bowl tickets and begin talk of the elusive fourth ring for Tom.

Here's how the drive went down: Tom took over at his own twelve-yard line, on my side of the field. On the first play, with running back Stevan Ridley standing several yards behind him, Tom directed backup tight end Michael Hoomanawanui, who has been filling in for Gronk, to go in motion and then park it in a blocking stance next to the right tackle. This showed a formation for a power run off the right side, just what any sane offensive coordinator and experienced quarterback would do on a first down at this point in the game, on a slippery night where you have the lead and you're deep in your own territory and need to avoid mistakes that could switch the momentum of the game. So Tom took the snap and leaned far to his right to hand off the ball. The entire offensive line exploded and blocked to the right. Ridley opened up his arms to take the ball, but Brady pulled it back for play-action: a fake running play. Tom shifted to his left and planted his feet behind his one remaining blocker, the stocky center Ryan Wendell. The quarterback opened up his hips and brought the football up high behind his head to throw. Back at his own five-yard line by then, Tom reared back, stepped forward with his left foot, and heaved the soppy wet ball nearly fifty yards in the air, in a spiral, to Danny Amendola, who was sprinting behind the Colts safety. This safety had slipped after biting hard on the fake run. Tom almost underthrew Amendola, but the receiver for his part adjusted to the ball in the air, cradled it in both arms, and would've perhaps gone the distance if he were not playing hurt with his sports-groin. Everyone in Gillette jumped to their feet and roared!

A couple plays later, several yards deeper into Colts territory, Tom now snapped the ball in the shotgun formation on a third down and seven. The Colts' leading pass rusher, Robert Mathis, forced him out of the pocket. Mathis had faked out the offensive tackle and was racing up the middle like a frothing werewolf. Uncharacteristic for Tom, who is hardly a scrambler, he escaped out the right side, stiff-armed another defensive lineman, and juked outside the pocket to fling it to Julian Edelman, who had found some open green in front of Tom's view.

Edelman caught the ball past the first-down marker, and got the crowd still more pumped up as he gave his first-down karate chop. All season long, it's been Julian Edelman. He's been almost as inspiring as Tom. From a seventh-round pick, to backup and injured, Edelman is now Brady's number one, most reliable target. He earned a one-thousand-yard, one-hundred-catch season. Sadly, in some ways, Pats fans have long forgotten Wes Welker.

Tom handed off for a short running play, and then on the next play was nearly strip-sacked by the same frothing Robert Mathis. But somehow he barely tucked it away and then, with Mathis grasping at his ankles, threw the football to the ground for an incompletion to avoid losing yardage. On third down, Brady lobbed it up toward Edelman on the sideline, who drew an easy pass interference call at the Colts five-yard line. Ridley banged it in for the touchdown. Tom and our offense were now four for four with touchdowns in the red zone and had been an extraordinary eight for twelve on third down. That drive ate up nearly five minutes of the third quarter.

In three big plays and a touchdown, Andrew Luck quickly put a pause on our victory party at the stadium, but we hit right back and then ran away with the game, quite literally, as LeGarrette Blount busted out a lumbering touchdown run for seventy-three yards in the fourth quarter and the true nail in the coffin. Again—I swear nearly all the big plays came in my direction—Blount broke through the line of scrimmage, made one linebacker miss, and then sprinted untouched all the way to my corner of the end zone. The running back watched himself up on the Jumbotron as he thundered ahead, aware of how far any defender was from him, so he pulled up and stopped just two steps over the goal line and cupped and thumped the ball down like you'd flip over a bucket of sand on the beach to make a castle. Blount's gesture shouted: "Touchdown, dammit!"

As Blount thundered toward us, it seemed everyone in the stadium had their hands up high to signal the touchdown. Bright yellow and blue and red rain jackets leaped up all across the stands. The family in front of me with their yellow coats hopped and shouted, and after Blount whumped the ball down and the referee signaled touchdown and the militia shot their rifles and the Patriots played their Bon Jovi "whoa, whoa, whoa" music, the two sons turned and hugged me. All three of us hugged together at the same time.

"Feel the joy! Feel the joy! Feel the joy!" hollered one of the brothers.

I shouted: "I know! I know! I know!"

The tall security guard came back up to me, patted my shoulder, and said: "You done being worried, my friend? You see, nothing to be worried about. I see you're cracking a smile now. One more ring, baby. You watch."

JANUARY 14 / 8:40 A.M.
FOXBOROUGH, MASSACHUSETTS

I'm in danger of a football overdose after the Patriots' 43–22 power-washing of the Colts. I simply cannot stop listening to radio and reading every possible prediction and analysis and argument as to who is better, Peyton or Tom. From dawn until late at night, from Sunday until kickoff, there is always a radio show with two or three guys talking about this one single upcoming AFC Championship game. One more win, and we're in the Super Bowl.

Sure, nearly all the discussion is inane, but on news radio there's talk this morning about the hundreds of thousands of Syrian refugees who have been basically under siege, caught between rebel armies. This is another thing that I've been trying to explain to Hoss. Pro sports is a distraction from our troubles, a safe place to funnel energies and emotions. "You can't just bury your head in the sand," he says. But I just can't take in all of the grim, awful, sad, violent, apocalyptic stories all the time, every hour. So I tune in to talk radio or click over to NFL.com and read about the meaningless, circular, purely semantic debate as to which quarterback, Tom or Peyton,

has more to gain if he could win another Super Bowl before retirement.

It's now five days until the game. This time it's in Denver, and the early forecast seems like it will be balmy, which seems the biggest strike against our chances. Last time it was cold and windy, in Foxborough. And we had Gronk then, and they didn't have their best tight end, Julius Thomas. But, then again, why not? The Broncos have some key guys hurt, too. We've still got Belichick and Brady. Tom has now been the starter for twelve seasons, and he's led his team to the conference championship game eight of those seasons, the most of any quarterback in history. He's won five conference championships already.

After being in the rain for so long at the Colts game, my Patriots hat actually looks pretty clean. #saveourmankycaps

---

JANUARY 15 / 2:40 P.M.
MANSFIELD, MASSACHUSETTS

I'm in the van with a coffee, after meeting Steve Grogan. He was the quarterback for the New England Patriots for nearly 150 games from the mid-'70s to 1990. I still have one of his cards from when I was collecting as a kid. He helped get our Patriots to the playoffs five times and all the way to an AFC Championship game, which we won—although then, in the franchise's first-ever appearance in the biggest game in 1986, we got walloped in the Super Bowl by the Chicago Bears. Grogan was an exceptionally mobile quarterback, as much of a scrambler as today's Cam Newton or Russell Wilson, and he set several records at the time for rushing yardage and running touchdowns by a quarterback for the Patriots and for the entire league. But Steve Grogan's legacy is really about his durability, his ability to play hurt, and the endurance to last for sixteen years in the NFL. He retired at nearly thirty-eight years old. Now Grogan owns a sporting goods business that he started with Rocky Marciano's brother. Grogan Marciano Sporting Goods is on a busy corner along a strip of blue-collar stores in a town only a few miles from Foxborough.

Among boxes of uniforms, baseball helmets, and walls of flaking paint, Steve talked with me at a table in the back room. I don't know if he could barely walk, as Sean Glennon told me, but Steve certainly moved carefully. He's tall, lanky, but certainly not someone you'd pick off the street and think *That guy must've been a pro football player*. Wearing small hearing aids, which clear the ringing in his ears that he attributes to contact on the field, Steve spoke softly, patiently, with still some native Kansan in his speech. He rarely pronounced his g's in a verb, so he'd say "runnin'" or "livin.'" He worked a piece of hard candy or a cough drop or a piece of gum in his mouth—I couldn't tell what it was exactly.

Steve Grogan had been retired for a decade when Tom joined the team, but Steve played with him a couple of times in charity basketball games.

"Was a real nice kid," Steve said. "But once they won the Super Bowl, he's kind of withdrawn from the public eye. And I don't see him. I might run into him briefly if I'm at the stadium for something, but no long conversations."

"You'd think there'd be a sort of Patriots quarterback club," I said.

"I think there's a mutual respect there, but when you're playing, you're focused on what you're doing. You don't want to be bothered talking small talk, even if it's a guy that played the game before. I remember going to banquets when I first came up here, Gino Cappelletti would be there, and Tom Yewcic, who was punter, Charlie Long, and Jim Nance, and all these guys from the '60s. But because I wasn't from around here I wasn't familiar with who they were and what they did, and it wasn't until later in my career that I found out they were some pretty good football players. But we did not have a lot of conversation because of the generation gap."

So Steve Grogan has never really had a genuine sit-down with Tom Brady. And Steve has never met Peyton Manning.

"The first thing is, I probably couldn't offer them any advice, because that is part of how the game has changed. These guys are making so much money nowadays. If they're halfway smart, which I think Brady and Manning are, they can do just about anything they want to do with the rest of their lives, whether it's television or kicking back and doing nothing. When I got out of the game that wasn't the case. I had to find a job. I had to make a living. I still had a family to raise. Tom's made a lot of good decisions, but marrying someone that makes twice as much as him, that's probably one of his best!"

We talked about how the players' association, pensions, and health insurance for players have evolved. Then Steve said that beyond player salaries, the second big change in the league was the proliferation of the passing attack, which was because of rule changes and the fans' desire for big scores. The Pats and most other teams in his era almost always ran the ball on first and second down.

The third big change, he explained, was with social media.

"These guys have no privacy whatsoever," Steve said. "Everybody knows what they're doing practically every minute of the day. When my kids were young we'd go to Kmart in the wintertime and let them run down the aisles to give them something to do. And people normally didn't bother us at all. If Tom Brady and Peyton Manning—and I'm not putting myself in their class—but they can't go anywhere without somebody knowing who they are and probably somebody wanting to talk to them or bother them or get an autograph or whatever."

Now, by the time Steve Grogan said this to me, several

other things had been piling up in recent weeks, such as, for example, I'd been trying to learn about how Tom engages with one of his primary charities, Best Buddies, which supports special-needs kids. It had taken me dozens of e-mails just to try to get a phone conversation with a person to *screen* me before I spoke with another someone at the nonprofit that works with Tom. Then, in the end, I never got to speak even with her. So these comments from Steve, although hardly new, stung a bit more than they have in the past, especially from someone like this ex-football player. All these people not writing me back, this feeling I'm hounding Tom, my MFL friends calling me a stalker—it's been sapping at my self-esteem. Honestly, I'm just about ready to give up. I think it might only be Uncle Frank that's keeping me going. I have another interview later today, and it's taken me six weeks to get this one, the correspondents regularly questioning my motives and making me feel pretty small. So Steve's comments here were another pin, maybe even a gash, to leak the air out of this adventure, one of many recently that have been seeping away my resolve and the pleasure in this whole pilgrimage. In my self-respect.

"It's starting to catch up with me," Steve continued, as I asked about his health. He is sixty years old.

"I'm starting to feel things on a regular basis." He laughed. "I wonder what or who hit me back then that made me feel this way today. When you're playing the game, you don't think about those kind of things. It's kind of like why they send young people to war. You think you're invincible. I'm not comparing football to war exactly, but you do go out and you fight battles with guys you love, and some guys get wounded —some guys get hurt so bad they never play again. You don't think about that when you're young." Steve drummed his fingers on the table and shifted in his chair. "At the same time, as I'm starting to get old and feel the bumps, the bruises, the bad backs, the bad necks, the bad knees, I'd go back and do it all over again. It was that much fun. How many people get to do a job they love?"

I wanted to ask him if he's seen Nick Nolte in *North Dallas Forty*, but that somehow seemed too close to home. I asked him instead if he'd watched the *Frontline* documentary.

"It's getting a little scary," he said. "I know some guys who are starting to have memory problems. I haven't reached that point yet. I'm glad they're doing something about it."

In a 1978 preseason game against the Oakland Raiders, Steve was the one who threw the ball to Darryl Stingley, a Patriots receiver who when stretching out for the catch was hit brutally in the air by Jack Tatum, a defensive back who embraced his mean reputation. Tatum lowered his shoulder into the defenseless Stingley at the precise angle—a hit that was legal in the '70s—that rendered Stingley an instant lifeless lump of limbs on the grass. Stingley was a quadriplegic for the rest of his life.

"That was very difficult to deal with," Steve said. "I've seen a lot of guys, hundreds of guys get hit in similar positions. All of them got up, get up, but for some reason, he didn't." He paused reverentially. "It hurt. It hurt me. It hurt our team for a long time. To know that it had happened to him. That was the toughest."

I, for my part, was nine years old at the time of that hit and at the apex, until now I guess, of my life as a football fan. I'm amazed I don't remember that event with Tatum and Stingley. Did my parents shield me from that story? My mother hated the Raiders and Jack Tatum, which struck me as an odd opinion from my mother at the time. I realize now that this is why she worried, quite genuinely, that I'd be paralyzed when I started playing.

I asked Steve Grogan: "What will you ask Tom when you do have a real conversation with him someday?"

"I would like to know about all the calls at the line of scrimmage—Manning's the worst—but what are all the things that Brady and Manning are talking about and pointing at and shouting out. We used to just call the play. You went up to the offensive line, hiked it, and you ran the play. And that was it. How do they disguise it so the defense doesn't pick all that up?"

Steve continued: "And I'd tell Tom to enjoy his family. He's got a couple young kids. That was some of my most enjoyable times, when I took them into the locker room, to meet the guys."

Steve shared a particular special game late in his career in which he came in as a backup and led the team for a comeback win. His five-year-old son was there that day, watching his dad for the first time. After the game, after his son saw him being interviewed for TV, Steve took his boy on his shoulders onto the field as the crowd shouted "Grogan! Grogan! Grogan!"

"Football can be all-consuming," Steve said, "especially when you play it at the level that Tom and Peyton do. But your family is more important than anything. Both of those two seem level-headed, though, perhaps two of the best quarterbacks there ever were, but also good people. I've met both of their dads. They come from good families.

"Now, I finished a couple years before I wanted to. I thought I had a couple more good years left as a backup, but the Patriots wanted me to retire, and they released me. I got out of bed the next morning, and I guess I hadn't realized for the sixteen years how much football and the pressure of football had consumed me. I felt like a weight had been lifted off my shoulders. I didn't have to go to the weight room. I didn't have to talk to anybody in the press. I didn't have anybody who was going to criticize me. I was just a regular guy. I was lucky to have a long career. It actually was kind of a good feeling. I knew it was time to move on to the rest of my life, and go find something I enjoyed doing."

5:45 P.M. / FOXBOROUGH, MASSACHUSETTS

I just came out of my appointment at the TB12 Sports Therapy Center, which is right along the outdoor mall, the main drag, outside Gillette Stadium. I met with Alex Guerrero, whom Tom has referred to in interviews as his "best friend" and his "body coach." First Alex was willing to speak with me, then he canceled, then he acquiesced. In the end, I paid an embarrassingly huge sum for a one-hour initial "consultation and treatment." I told Alex the truth, that I wanted to ask about how he uses Tom's story to motivate and train his athletes, to hear how he and Tom started this facility, and to get my own evaluation as I heal my back and return to running more seriously, perhaps even run a marathon again someday.

The facility inside had a tall reception desk, manned by a friendly woman named Melanie. Through a frosted-glass door was a hallway. Inside to the right was a series of clean, white examination rooms with names such as "Focus" and "Determination." To the left was a stretch of green artificial turf with lines painted on the surface. From the ceiling hung nets in adjustable permutations for, say, hitting baseballs or throwing footballs. There were a couple of treadmills, yoga mats, a basketball in one corner. Beyond the stretch of turf, on the left, was a room with computers, presumably to watch video of athletic motion. Apparently Tom comes here every day. Can he just walk here from the stadium? Is there an underground tunnel so no one bugs him?

I first read about Alex Guerrero and the TB12 Sports Therapy Center in last summer's issue of *Men's Health*, which featured Tom on the cover. Alex has been helping the quarterback in recent years keep his body in shape with natural, progressive, and even unconventional methods of flexibility, strength training, and diet designed for the long term. On a daily basis, Alex works on Tom's flexibility and his recovery, in collaboration with Tom's personal throwing coach and Tom's personal chef.

Alex is a smaller man, with thin, fashionable glasses. He looked fit, but certainly not like a weightlifter or a marathoner. On TV, I've seen him on the sidelines sometimes, even in the locker room after a game. He didn't quite know what to do with me this afternoon. I tried to explain my mission.

"I just get so many requests for interviews about Tom," he said. "About one a day now." He said that Tom and he had planned to start this fitness center after Tom retired, but they kept getting so many questions about Tom's training methods, and his teammates wanted help, and it just became the right time to set something up here in Foxborough. It's well known, and Tom has said often, that he hopes to play well into his forties.

"Age is just a number," Alex said.

I told him about how I've been getting back into running myself at age forty-three, and I want to try to keep healthy proactively. Particularly with my back. I had blown out my running shoes in California, my toes stuck straight through after the run through the city, so I brought today what I've been jogging with in the last week, my "Euro-sneaks," as Lenny calls them—an odd pair of vaguely European indoor sport shoes I once bought at a discount store. Alex wasn't especially impressed by these, nor with my black socks, but I just hadn't had a chance to buy a new pair of running shoes.

Alex set me up on a high-tech treadmill with another trainer. The man set up a little camera behind me that captured a steady, thoroughly unflattering video of my butt, hamstrings, and calves in motion. I ran first barefoot and then with the Euro-sneaks. The trainer talked me through a series of complex observations of my running motion and foot placement and muscle strain, which I came very close to understanding more than once. He printed out some fancy color sheets with graphics and numbers and presented them to Alex, who went over them with me, and I came even closer to understanding some of their conclusions, but at this point, now an hour after the appointment, all I've retained is that I run awkwardly when I'm barefoot, something about my left leg, which is slightly corrected when I wear my Euro-sneaks.

Alex explained to me about how professional athletes stretch, which actually was pretty informative. Apparently no one does the sort of static stretches that I was taught growing up, holding one position and steadily increasing how far you go. Nowadays, the athletes actually don't stretch extraordinarily hard before workouts.

"You think a cheetah stretches before sprinting?" Alex asked me. I wanted to ask him how many cheetahs he knew that sit and write e-mails for five hours at a stretch. But his general premise made a lot of sense, and it explains why whenever you see the Patriots on television in some lineup of stretching, they're doing so lightly, actively—just sort of wobbling their hips around or skipping and jogging before a serious workout. He spoke about the importance of hydration in order to keep muscles pliable.

Alex had me lie on a padded therapy table and probed my leg muscles with his fingers. With one touch, he told me my right hip flexor is weaker than the left. He ground three fingers into my left leg, just above the quad.

"Your muscles build through trauma," he said.

"Well, that certainly hurt," I said, my eyes tearing up.

After I changed back into my street clothes, Alex came in to say good-bye. I asked him if we could talk more about Tom, and how he and the quarterback motivate the other athletes that come in here, including the amateur ones.

"After the Super Bowl," he said. "We can talk again after the Super Bowl."

On my way out, Melanie offered me some bottled water.

"Alex *did* talk about hydration," I said.

The water bottle has a custom "TB12" label. Tom Brady springwater. He wants me to drink a lot of water. To drink responsibly.

JANUARY 16 / 3:25 P.M.
MYSTIC, CONNECTICUT

I can get nothing done besides listen to talk radio and scroll the websites, trying to find some clue to the Patriots-Broncos championship game. I can't tell if I like it or not when a pundit predicts a Pats win. Most are taking the Broncos at home. A little over seventy-one hours until kickoff. Breaking news: "Tom Brady Seen with Cough Drop: Too Sick to Play?"

I spoke to my uncle Frank, who said it would be best if I got to Sports Authority Field in Denver before the game to try to meet Tom. To do something tragic.

"That's really the only appropriate culmination of your self-loathing project," Uncle Frank said. "Now that we know he's not going to meet with you, even in the off-season, you've just got to figure a way that you get shot with a bullet, but it's sort of sad, too—that you are trying to do something that isn't violent. You are running to deliver to him the secret play to beat the Broncos—you thought of it, discovered it, while thinking about the game when you were eating breakfast and you scribbled the bit of strategic genius frantically on a napkin, but you tucked it in a black envelope and wrote 'Tom' with one of your daughter's silver glittery markers, because that's all you had around the house. You sneak into the corridor that leads out to the stadium, just before the teams are ready to take the field, but a new security guy sees you. The man is hung over from amphetamines and his contact lenses are bothering him, making his vision fuzzy (but he also hates Jews, which will come out in the investigation). He sees you, barely, and thinks the envelope you're clutching, as you run urgently toward Brady, is a gun. The security guy empties his pistol into your belly and takes you out. And you're left face down in a pool of your own blood, the key play in your hand. Something like that. That's all you have left really."

"Do I die?" I asked.

"Do you want a sequel?" Uncle Frank said.

JANUARY 17 / 10:20 P.M.
MYSTIC, CONNECTICUT

I haven't quite mustered the courage to call in to a radio show, but I did write in to *Patriots Football Weekly* asking about what life might be like for Brady after football. They answered my question both online and on their television show.

Online, one of the Patriots writers, named Eric Scalavino, who is about my age, called my question a "profound one." I hit a nerve with him, because he replied this way about Tom and Peyton, in one of the longest responses I've ever seen him post—and this is only part of it:

> For both their sakes, I'd like to see them exit gracefully, which might mean doing so before either is mentally prepared to do so. I feel pity for guys like Brady (who seem to have it all, yes), when they say, as he has often, that he doesn't know what he'll do with himself after football. That he wants to play as long as possible because that's all he knows. It is truly sad to hear that. Sure, he

loves football. So do a lot of us. But there is a great big world out there with infinite possibilities. Brady and Manning and other NFL players are forced to spend nearly every waking hour during their careers focusing on nothing but this game. That makes for a very boring, one-dimensional person. So, it's understandable that he knows not what he'll do when he retires. But trust me, there's WAY more to life than football. For instance, they could take music lessons, learn to cook, travel the world, go back to school, start a charitable foundation, volunteer at their church or other civic organization . . . the list goes on and on and on. Who knows, one of these activities just might be more enjoyable to them than football ever was! You know what they say . . . Life begins at 40. Hopefully, Manning and Brady embrace that philosophy.

On the *Patriots Football Weekly* television show, analyst Andy Hart said: "I think Brady can do anything he wants. He's capable of anything."

Tom, as we pass the ball back and forth, what are you thinkin'? You can tell me. . . .

My concern after the responses from the *Patriots Football Weekly* guys, however, is that they used my real name online. Does Pressman James read everything? Crazy list.

Meanwhile, Tom's had two extra-long midweek press conferences in a row.

"When you play against one of the best teams in the league, there's very little margin for error," he answered. "Peyton's a great player, they got a great team, one of the best offenses in history. So that means we got to go out there and score some points."

One reporter chimed in to say that an annual NFL poll

claims that Tom is the least liked NFL quarterback among fans. "Why do you think?"

"Well, there's probably a lot of reasons," Tom laughed.

"Some have suggested jealousy of not just your football success, but the kind of life you have off the field."

"What kind of life do I have off the field?" Tom joked. The press corps laughed heartily. Tom added: "I guess you'll just have to ask those people that you polled. But yes, you're right, there's nothing I'd rather do than play football for the New England Patriots. And, yes, I have a great family."

Forty hours until kickoff.

JANUARY 18 / 10:15 A.M.
MYSTIC, CONNECTICUT

Just got off the phone with Seth Wickersham, the ESPN feature writer I interviewed last summer. He was on his way to catch a plane to Denver.

Seth spoke about the season and commented on how Tom, with his new throwing coach, has developed a longer follow-through. He had talked to Tom about it before the pre-season game against Philadelphia, and Seth noticed it again in our most recent win against Indianapolis, especially when Tom threw that game-cementing long ball to Danny Amendola. Seth said that Tom explained that now it's all muscle memory. He doesn't even have to think about it.

"I thought that was pretty amazing," Seth told me. "That somebody at age thirty-six can change something so fundamental in his throwing motion, like a golfer changing his swing. And have it hold up, when he's got chaos all around him. Peyton Manning's motion hasn't changed since college. Whereas Brady's throw is now drastically different. It's indicative of his craft, as to how Brady keeps improving. Brady is more driven than ever to keep playing."

Seth isn't sure about tomorrow's outcome. "I think Denver will win: they have better weapons and they're at home, but New England has the better overall team. I could see the Patriots winning. Either way, it's going to be nuts."

Sixteen hours and fifteen minutes.

JANUARY 19 / 2:50 P.M.
MYSTIC, CONNECTICUT

As soon as my eyelids opened this morning, I was nervous. I'm at the Pier 27 Lounge now. Kickoff in ten minutes. I'm no longer nervous: I'm terrified.

All week it's been Manning-Brady XV. Manning is meat and potatoes. Brady is haute cuisine. Manning is a Bud Light. Brady is a margarita. Manning has been groomed to be the greatest quarterback since birth. Brady has had to scrap and struggle. Manning has had to make do with multiple coaches on two different teams—without the genius that is Belichick. Brady has had to make do with no-name receivers on offense year after year, with the genius that is Belichick cruelly cutting all of Brady's supporting stars. Manning always chokes in the playoffs. Brady has been choking in the playoffs in recent years. Manning has the better statistics in almost every category. Except in team wins, where Brady has a better regular-season and postseason percentage. Brady is 10–5 in head-to-head matchups, and 2–1 when they've met in the playoffs. But the playoff winner has always been the home team. Manning wears number eighteen. Brady wears number twelve. Thus sportswriters have dubbed this "The War of 18–12."

I did my job this morning. I once again broke my record for my running route. I was really nervous before I began, because unlike the sunny and sixty degrees there in Denver this afternoon, it's bitter cold and windy here in New England. I still only had my Euro-sneaks to sprint over occasional patches of ice. I did my wobbly hip flexor stretches and hydrated with my Tom Brady springwater that I'd saved for this run. But what if I failed? The Pats need me.

Tom, are you aware that most people approach a moment of challenge by thinking What if I fail? *When you're in that tall corridor about to enter the field as one of the last true gladiators, you really don't think that way, do you?*

So I dawdled and stretched some more. I wore my number-twelve jersey and my cap and my black balaclava and my eye-black. Then I just did it. I pressed start on my watch and bolted hard immediately, setting a pace that I knew I couldn't possibly keep up. What if I don't break the record, I worried, sucking in the frozen air. I felt slow. I sprinted until I thought I would vomit, and then I kept going, kept digging deep, pulling my balaclava down off my head as I warmed up, and kept running, and even up the third and steepest hill I lashed myself up and over the pavement. Felt the burn in my thighs.

"Now this is the hill whose ass I am going to kick!" I growled to myself. "Do not slow down. I am going to set this record." I pounded on the downhill after passing the library, trying not to peek at my watch, but just sprinting and sprinting. Breathing smoothly, relaxing my shoulders, using my arms for more power. "I am going to set this record." And I came down the hill back to our house and pressed the stop button on my watch as I fell on the ice-crunch grass of our front lawn. I dry heaved. I rolled on my back and looked at the face of the watch.

I *killed* the old record by fifteen seconds.

So, there is a chance today. I've done my job. We just might beat these Broncos this afternoon. Supposedly Brady rewards himself with ice cream made from avocados and other natural ingredients. I got to Pier 27 and ordered myself a large meatball sub and a Guinness.

The Pier 27 Lounge is packed, the thickest I've ever seen it. The crowd feels like it's mostly Pats fans. "Everyone is here, for the pizza and beer," sings Nick Name. Loud Brady Lady and her husband are here, as is Mr. Little. Dolphins Guy and Dr. No-No and even Steelers Alley seem to be rooting for the Pats, which is a surprise. This leaves Gangly John a lone, pacing wolf, but he's not one to shy from this sort of challenge. He has replaced his Elway number seven with a Manning number eighteen. Gangly Peyton. Hoss and Lenny said they're going to come pretty soon, too.

I got my little table with the best view of the biggest screen. I got here about an hour and a half before the game, just to be sure. Dolphins Guy said: "Don't worry, I'd have saved your spot for you."

If I weren't so concerned about the game, I would take that as a very good omen. But even though we've beaten the Broncos before, it's at their place now, and we're a limping army. It's Rocky vs. Ivan Drago. Maybe, just maybe, we might just take another run at the Super Bowl, Tom. Crash through this final door, and you'll be the only man in history to be the starting quarterback of a Super Bowl six times. And now here it is. Denver has won the toss. They deferred. So the Pats are receiving. Brady will take the field first. C'mon, Tommy. C'mon, now.

10:45 P.M.

"How you doing?" Lenny said.

"You all right, buddy?" Hoss said, patting my shoulder.

"It's amazing how sudden it is," I said. "Just like that. And now it's over."

We ordered another round of beers and stared at the last lonely slices of pizza. We could spread out now, as most of the Pats-Broncos people had left and only a few were here at Pier 27 to watch the other conference championship, Seattle vs. San Francisco.

"Brady didn't play that bad," Lenny said.

"Right? I mean, Tommy was good, but not amazing. That's the thing. That's what Steve Grogan and Seth Wickersham and Sean Glennon and everyone else said: Tommy had to be perfect to win this game. You look who he was throwing to. They shut down Edelman, and he still got a couple passes to him, but then it was trying to get the ball to blocking tight ends, to a hobbled Dobson, to wide receivers you see more on special teams. To Austin Collie."

"There was that deep throw to Edelman."

"Yeah, that one. That one. If he'd only thrown that two feet softer, not overthrown him, that could've been the long-ball touchdown off that play action, that would've changed our whole game."

"Was it the warm day, the higher elevation?"

"Don't know."

"Listen, 26–16 isn't that bad," Hoss said.

"It really wasn't that close, though," I said. "Denver was just better."

"Was there a single turnover in the game?"

"Nope, not one interception, not one fumble for either side. No big special-teams plays. Just Denver driving slowly each time. They had two drives over seven minutes long. Mr. Little said they were Peyton's longest drives all season."

"Peyton is usually good for a couple interceptions in big games."

"No interceptions today, I guess. I mean, the Patriots didn't sack him even once. Barely touched his uniform."

"I'm thinking about that one play early in the second half, when Belichick went for it on fourth and two at the Broncos thirty. And Pot Roast for the Broncos, that big-belly lineman, just juked Mankins and came in and clobbered Tom before he even had a chance to look up."

"At least Brady didn't complain about that. Just kept it cool."

"Yeah, Tommy's still got it as a leader, at least. Didn't get all Bobby Layne on his lineman."

Hoss lowered his voice: "Hey, who's the tall guy in the corner with the Broncos jersey?"

"That's Gangly John," I said. "He's in heaven. He's been pretty good, considering."

"He can't stop smiling."

"Is he stoned?"

"Mile High, buddy."

"Good one."

"That's nothing. He's being good. I thought he'd be rubbing it in all our faces now."

"The thing I really can't believe," Lenny said, reluctantly picking up another slice, "is that Aqib Talib got hurt in the first quarter. No wonder we couldn't stop the pass."

"Again, right?! Another AFC Championship and our best cornerback is out in the first half."

"And another big playoff game without Gronk."

"And Talib blindsided by Wes Welker, no less, the turncoat! Welker was the one who took out Talib."

"Remember when Tommy ran it in for a touchdown?"

"They gave it to him in garbage time."

"It was still sweet."

"I'm sorry, buddy."

"It happens so suddenly. It might be his last chance."

"Remember after college when we were all living together in that house on Bruggeman Place?" Hoss said. "The kitchen clock on the wall died one morning, and you just taped a drawing of the hands of a clock over it and wrote 'It's later than you thought.'"

"Of course I do. We kept it like that for like three years."

"It was all we needed to know."

"Frankly, gentlemen," Lenny said, "as a New England fan, I prefer this. I'd rather they lose in the AFC Championship than in the Super Bowl. It's harder somehow when it's almost there. If you don't get as close, it doesn't hurt as much."

"Just like that. The dream is over," I said.

"I'm sorry," Hoss said. "Maybe it's about time to stop stalking this guy anyway. To stop trying to meet the alpha ape and just be happy you are who you are."

"You're writing for Hallmark now?" Lenny said to Hoss. "You're the one constantly bitching about how there is nothing good about growing old."

"That's right," Hoss said. "And I still don't know anything good about it. But our little Brady boyfriend here has shown us something, anyway. At least he's gone out and tried to make things to look forward to, for us all to look forward to. Even if he's failed."

"Tom's failed *him*," Lenny said.

"Listen," Hoss continued, looking at me. "You've given yourself an adventure. Seriously. And it's a reminder that we're lucky enough that we can give ourselves these things. I mean, if you concede that when you get older you don't get any wiser —"

"Just more cynical," Lenny said.

"Exactly. You just get more cynical. So Tom Brady has absolutely nothing that he can feel bad about himself. He's perfect and lives the perfect life and never does or says anything stupid and he's got the perfect genes and is making perfect children. But at least no one slaps a W or an L on *your* forehead after every week."

"I got an L on my mission to meet Tom," I said.

"No one thought you'd get this far."

"Are you talking about me or the Pats?"

"I'm talking about your hippie van."

"Middle age is disappointment, by definition."

"At least you tried."

"That's what we tell third graders."

"We also tell third graders not to eat their own snot, and that's useful advice."

"He's still the greatest there ever was."

"Not if Peyton wins this Super Bowl."

"Whatever it is, someone will come around someday and be better than you. Fulfill your dream better than you."

"They don't tell you that in third grade."

"Not in America."

"They should."

"You know what else they don't tell you about in third grade?"

"What?"

"Athletic pubalgia."

JANUARY 29 / 8:10 A.M.
MYSTIC, CONNECTICUT

A new semester starting. I'm on my way to drag myself to stand in front of a new class.

While the Broncos get ready to meet the Seahawks for the Super Bowl at the Meadowlands, outside frigid New York City, the paparazzi posted photographs of Tom in surf shorts and Gisele in a string bikini paddleboarding in the Bahamas.

"Mystic Backyard Boats Now Repairs Paddleboards."

I found this on my shelves this weekend, a story I remembered reading in graduate school. A character in Anton Chekhov's 1893 novella *An Anonymous Story* says: "But this is the question, why are we worn out? Why are we, at first so passionate, so bold, so noble, and so full of faith, complete bankrupts at thirty or thirty-five? Why does one waste in consumption, another put a bullet through his brains, a third seek forgetfulness in vodka and cards, while the fourth tries to stifle his fear and misery by cynically trampling underfoot the pure image of his fair youth? Why is it that, having once fallen, we do not try to rise up again, and, losing one thing, do not seek something else? Why is it?"

FEBRUARY 4 / 2:30 P.M.
MYSTIC, CONNECTICUT

When I picked up Alice from preschool this afternoon, I was collecting her backpack, and Alice ran off to get the paper fireman she made to show me. Her teacher said: "Alice is so lucky to have her daddy."

She has no idea how moving that was, how important that was for me.

FEBRUARY 8 / 9:30 P.M.
MYSTIC, CONNECTICUT

It's a week after the Super Bowl. Young Russell Wilson, his second year in the league, led his Seahawks to a dominant one-sided drubbing of the Denver Broncos. It was over in the first quarter. Manning was mauled, thumped, embarrassed by a Seattle defense who seemed to be playing at a faster speed. I didn't go to Pier 27, but went and watched the game with my dad.

I just got off the phone this morning with Heidi Gilbert, the animator in Los Angeles who won the NFL "Together We Make Football" contest to go to the Super Bowl. They arranged a video conversation with her and Tom, from wherever he and his family were staying in the Bahamas. Heidi told me that part of the inspiration she drew from Tom was how competitive he is, and that this gave her permission to appreciate this part of herself that she'd previously thought of as a negative trait.

Heidi told me that before the video chat she was nervous that she "would just turn into a ball of tears" when she first saw him on the screen, that she wouldn't be able to compose herself and figure out what to say. "This was my one chance," she told me. She had a sheet of notes in front of her. But after some initial awkwardness, it all worked out more comfortably than she expected.

Tom broke the ice by talking about how amazed he was that the satellite video even worked from a Caribbean island. He was wearing a black hat—I think his "TB12" brand—and a plain gray T-shirt.

"I'm terrible at electronics," he told her.

Then he congratulated Heidi on winning the contest, apologizing he didn't meet her in person when she was in Foxborough. Heidi had gone to that same frozen Broncos game that I did, before she won the contest. She and Tom joked about that night game in Gillette, about how even he was cold.

"We just came up a little short this last one against the Broncos," Tom told her. "I'm still bummed out."

"Me, too," Heidi told him.

Heidi then made sure to tell Tom her story, to thank him for inspiring her to keep trying as an artist: "You really gave me my hope back, when I didn't have any."

Tom nodded humbly. Said he was proud of her: "The thing is, no one is going to believe in you, unless you believe in yourself. That's the first thing."

But Tom. What if you don't—what if you cannot believe in yourself?

At the end of the interview, Heidi asked for a virtual high five. "He seemed to love that," Heidi told me this morning. "He was like *Yeah-yeah*." (There had been a whole funny story this past season about how TV cameras kept catching Brady left hanging by his teammates when he went up for high fives on the sideline.)

"What did you wish you could've asked him?" I said to Heidi this morning.

"I guess I would've asked him what inspired *him*. What helped him through all the adversity he faced."

Heidi finished by telling me: "I was so worried. Have you heard that expression 'Never meet your heroes'? Man, what if this was going to just shatter my illusion of who he is? It wasn't like that at all. He was just a super nice guy. It felt very normal talking to him."

FEBRUARY 26 / 1:15 P.M.

FOXBOROUGH, MASSACHUSETTS

I am in the reception area of the New England Patriots offices inside Gillette Stadium, waiting for my meeting with the Pressman Stacey James. One last drive.

I took the elevator, which opened to a receptionist behind a black desk. She scanned my driver's license, took a photograph of me with a digital camera, and then printed out a dated photo ID for me to stick on my chest. She directed me to wait in this spotless corporate circular room with glass displays of trophies, Super Bowl ephemera, old Patriots jerseys going back to 1960, and television screens showing clips of playoff games and Super Bowls. I want to take a photograph, but would that appear suspicious? Within glass display cases is a Tom Brady MVP ball, a *Sports Illustrated* cover with Brady, and a Wheaties cereal box with Brady and a couple of other players.

A pizza deliveryman walks out of the elevator, checks in with the receptionist, and then goes through the door to the inner sanctum. Another man comes in, no bag, no jacket, waits opposite me for a while, and then is met at the door by someone I don't recognize.

I've prepared a general list of questions for Pressman James, but most important is to make a good impression, and then maybe, just maybe, he'll say something like: *Well, let me talk to Tom one more time. He's actually at the stadium this afternoon, working out with Julian. You have time right now?* Or maybe he'll say: *How flexible are you regarding location next week? Could you travel to his new place in LA?*

Oh, that's him! The Pressman Stacey James in the flesh. Here we go.

Back at the house now.

Stacey welcomed me through the door and led me to his office, which was beside that of one of the editors of *Patriots Football Weekly*, a face I recognized, and opposite a small field of cubicles with people working on computers.

He sat me opposite his desk. I brought out my pad and recorder. Stacey wore a button-down shirt. My guess is he's in his late forties. We have about the same amount of gray on the sides. He has blue, busy eyes. His office is decorated with Patriots memorabilia and family photographs behind him. A television playing the NFL network hangs from the ceiling so he can look up to it from his computer. With the draft moved back until May this year and the Super Bowl almost a month in the rearview mirror, there's very little news in the pro football world right now.

Stacey has been with the team since 1993, beginning as the assistant director of public relations. As he spoke with me, he broke off several times to read an e-mail or a text on his phone, and he occasionally responded to them. Twice he spoke to me about something he said as being off the record, and I won't write them down here, but in both cases these comments seemed innocuous. He bracketed these points clearly with "off the record" and then "back on the record." I'm sure he didn't share anything actually sensitive with me.

I've been writing to him now in some fashion nearly once a week for over four months. But when I sat down he did not exactly say the words *And you are again?* but it was in his face. It wasn't rude or unkind, it was simply, *I'm busy, remind me your scene again?*

I summarized who I was.

He began: "I don't know if I replied with this, but Tom has a way that I now reply to the number of requests that he gets: 'Tom Brady is going to do what Tom Brady does best. He's going to pass.'"

"Funny," I laughed.

"Yeah. And most people respond: 'Hey, that's great.' From a PR perspective, I see the opportunities that come his way and think, wow, what great publicity. What great PR for him and the Patriots. *And, Tom, I would love for you to consider this, this, and this.* His perspective has evolved over time. It used to be, when he was very young and he had just won the Super Bowl, all these opportunities came out of the woodwork, and Brady wanted to make sure the team got the credit, not the individual. He's always been concerned with the inclusion of others."

In those early years of massive success, Brady faithfully echoed the messaging of Belichick and the Kraft family by responding to invitations for award ceremonies and advertising offers by saying that he would prefer if the team captains were also flown out to attend the event, or that he'd rather his entire offensive line join him, for example, in a credit card TV commercial.

"Even then," Stacey said. "Tom was very selective in the things he would make time for. It was fun to see from my desk that we had in the most important position someone who wanted to involve teammates that way. I can observe from afar—I don't know the situation in every other market—but I can observe other examples where it's not the case. I've been very fortunate to have, in my twenty years here, Drew Bledsoe and Tom Brady as our two quarterbacks. We couldn't have two better faces of the franchise. Tom really hasn't changed a lot since he first arrived as a fourth-string quarterback. He was polished then, but he's also matured, too. He's learned. There's a story out there that one day young Tom Brady was in the car with his family driving around the San Francisco Bay area and he saw Dwight Clark—I'm pretty sure it was Dwight Clark—in the next car over. Tom can remember his reaction when he was a boy, what that felt like to see the wide receiver that had grabbed that famous catch from Joe Montana. He remembers the perspective of the fan. And in his early years Tom relayed that anecdote, to help him understand why people react the way they do when *he* was out in public. The way he was in his youth."

Stacey was not terse or guarded. He chuckled at times. He rarely gave much room for questions, which was fine by me.

"I see him when the cameras aren't on," Stacey continued. "I see him with the kids we bring in from Make-a-Wish, or I see him with somebody who has been so eager to meet him. It's not a switch for when the camera goes on. He's not phony. He's always polished. He's always on. He's always that genuine person who looks you in the eyes, shakes your hand, and asks you a question that engages you in a conversation, and you are certain that he will remember your name the next time he meets you."

"And does he?" I asked.

"I've seen him meet people again when, you know, he'll have that void or loss for what to say, but he always has a great save and will pull out something like 'Oh, do you know Laura?' And then they'll go into a conversation. He always finds some connection. He's very good about making each person feel special and feel remembered."

"What is the scale of requests you get for Tom's time? Is it daily?"

Stacey paused to answer an e-mail in a few quick keystrokes. He explained the height of requests for Tom's time was during the Super Bowl years. Tom did everything once — *Saturday Night Live*, Letterman, Leno, Disney. He was a judge for Miss USA. Once he got married and had children, though, Tom told Stacey that family and football were the two most important things to him. He didn't want to do anything anymore that took away from either of those two.

"So that really wipes out a lot. Unless it falls within his media commitment obligations, it's probably no. What happens is that when he does do an interview, people say, 'Whoa, hey, did you see Tom Brady on Fox? What about us?' So after any interview request he grants, we'll get a new flood of requests. Each off-season he'll do one or two endorsements. More as a model than as a spokesperson. We've seen him also do one annual long interview. *GQ*, *American Way*, *Men's Health*. Typically only one. I think his agent handles most of those now. When he started doing less, when he started *passing*, the requests went down. It's not as crazy as you would think now."

"Do you discuss *all* the opportunities with him?"

"There are a lot things now that I know he won't do. I set a very low expectation. I guess I show him the overwhelming majority of requests. I might batch them up a little bit. Or if it's more random, I'll send him one here and there. I'll say during the season: 'Here's what you're obligated to do, and, oh, by the way, here are four other requests this week.' Most of the time he'll say 'I'll pass on those,' but every now and then we'll cherry-pick one, or there will be a relationship thing, or someone will get a chance to ask him directly, and we'll say 'Okay, we'll do this.'"

"Can I ask if you gave him my request?"

"Yes."

"You did?"

"I did."

"Thank you. I know it's a little bit oddball."

I wasn't sure how I felt about this answer, because at a certain point, if Tom knows I've been asking, no does mean no. The play clock has run out. The pilgrimage is over. The mission is officially a failure. I hadn't realized this until I asked, but I hoped that he might tell me that he was waiting to meet me before he sent it to Tom. Or something like that. (But maybe, as I thought driving home, maybe Stacey James wasn't telling me the truth then? Maybe he never did give it to him?)

Stacey filled in the awkward pause: "When I ask Tom to do some of these really great community relations opportunities, we try to do it in the way that provides the best experience for the child, or fan, or whoever it is, in a way that takes the least amount of time from his routine. On a Saturday Tom does this. On a Friday he does this. On Wednesday he does this. For example, one of the things we started to do some time ago was to bring multiple kids from Make-a-Wish who have requested to meet Tom to come out to a practice on a Saturday when the team does a walk-through the day before a game. Tom liked to grab a few of his teammates, and that has grown to be the whole team comes over now and says hi to these kids and spends fifteen, twenty minutes, interacting, playing, having fun with these kids who have life-threatening illnesses. The kids think it's the greatest thing ever. They meet the whole team, and Robert Kraft and Bill Belichick. Tom's happy to do it. But we have made it convenient from a timing standpoint. And it can be impactful for those kids. He has been the perfect spokesperson for the organization."

Stacey paused to call someone to find out about the location of his two o'clock meeting. Again, Pressman James was not rude or unkind. He was busy, he let me feel his busy-ness, but he did talk to me, he did invite me here, and there seems to be very little in it for him, for the New England Patriots to gain, by responding to an annoying request from some random writer. Did Stacey see this half hour with me as his own charity visit?

I, meanwhile, realized with no small amount of shame what I should have understood nearly a year ago before I concocted this pilgrimage: that I'd rather have some kid from Make-a-Wish have a catch and a conversation with Tom before I ever do. That my pursuit has not only been self-demeaning, "self-loathing" as Uncle Frank says, but even somewhat selfish.

Stacey let me squeeze in a few more questions until the next appointment came to pick him up. When I asked him about the crazy list, if there was such a thing, if *I* had been placed on such a list, things got weird. Because it felt as the words came out as if I were seeking to find some sort of opening in security. I wasn't able to phrase the question without it sounding icky. Like I actually am a stalker of the pasted magazine letters variety.

I said: "Is there for celebrities—well, um, someone like me envisions that there is, like, Tom Brady has at any given time a hundred people that are literally stalking him, really trying immorally to have contact with him in some way. Is there *a list*? Where 'Oh, that guy, he's a—' and they send it out, zap, to all the people someone like that would be likely to contact."

Stacey looked at me and said softly: "I do not know what that means."

"I guess I'm envisioning, let's say, presumably a celebrity at the level of Brady has, like, people that are desperate to get next to him. There'd be some system. Let's say there are three hundred people that want an interview with Brady every year, or every week, I still don't even know."

"Right."

"We're all going to go through the same channels. I'm going talk to coaches in Ann Arbor. I'm going to go to his high school coach. I'm going to badger you. Is there like *a crazy list*, where you would say, 'Y'know this guy is pretty sketchy, and if he contacts you I would not respond to him—'"

"Oh, no. I don't do that. We had something just recently where the Celtics reached out to me and asked, 'Have you been contacted by this guy?' I said, 'As a matter of fact, yeah, we're meeting with him tomorrow.' And they said, 'This was not what we thought it was. Just wanted to pass it along.' It was someone who was speaking in half-truths. There is some industry sharing. But I've never once had a bad experience with a media person where then I've felt obligated to respond to a bunch of people to say 'Hey, if this person calls you, stay away.'"

The man for the two o'clock appointment, wearing a tie, came to the door and said "Ready?" without looking at me.

Stacey looked relieved. I was disappointed it had ended awkwardly.

"Is that enough?" he said to me.

"You know, never," I said. "But I really appreciate your time."

The Pressman Stacey James went over to a young woman in a cubicle. Asked her to walk me out. The receptionist then asked for my sticker ID back. I went down the elevator and into the cold, giving a nod and a weak smile to the construction safety guy who was still standing outside in the same place as when I went in.

The van started right up and drove me home. That was probably the best part of my day. Turning that key and having the faithful old van start right up. (I had a jumper battery standing by, just in case.) When I got home tonight I tried to open the van's sliding door, but it was so cold that it was frozen shut. I was angry. I tried to bang it with my fist, which broke the handle in half. Now I can't open that door at all, even from the inside. I cursed the cars going too fast on our road.

My mission to meet Tom Brady is over now, without having arrived much of anywhere. And I feel worse about myself and my prospects than I did even last summer. This entire quest to try to meet Brady was a boy's errand, and I felt it on the drive home with a teenager's depth of disappointment. I know still almost nothing about Tom Brady and less about myself.

"If you had reached out to talk to the president," the Pressman James said at one point this afternoon, "would you expect to get that audience? You, as a journalist?"

"Um, well, certainly not," I said.

"Right. Well, maybe some people have the same expectation."

Mr. Brady, would you be appalled that he put you in the same tier of power and importance as the president of the United States? Or would you sigh, shrug, and recognize that it is sad but probably true—that it's all not about relevance or power or intellect to Americans, but it's usually more about athletics, about celebrity?

This morning Alice and I bundled up and went walking for our bagel. She asked for her daily story. So I made up one about a peddler who wants to meet the king. The peddler is sad, and he feels like talking to the king will help him out somehow. He's not even sure why. So the peddler goes up to the castle and knocks, and they tell him *no* and *no* again, but he keeps trying, day after day. Because that's what you do, you try hard. One winter afternoon a cook in a ragged coat comes out from around the side of the castle and tells the peddler that he has been banished from the royal kitchen because he has a stomachache and can no longer work because he is so ill. Would he help him? The peddler leads the sick cook home, where he, his wife, and their daughter take him in. They welcome the cook in their shack, let him sleep there for a week, and the little family apologizes that they have no money to take him to the doctor. They give him soothing soups and teas. Soon the cook is feeling better, and one morning he reveals that he is, in fact, the king himself! The king wanted to find out what the peddler was really like and felt like he couldn't do it with the crown on his head. Regal knights on beautiful horses brought the peddler and his family back to the castle to meet the queen. The peddler and his family were showered with gifts and given spiritually fulfilling and profitable jobs in the castle. And they all lived happily ever after with beloved animals and really cool old cars and boats.

"Can you tell me a real story?" Alice said. "That would never happen. I want a monster story tomorrow."

"Why wouldn't that happen?" I said.

"Just wouldn't, Daddy. The king would get his own doctor to fix his stomachache. Kings have their own doctors."

"Maybe the king wanted to find out about the peddler?"

"Daddy, do you know how many peddlers have been knocking on the king's door? He's already found out about peddlers."

"But maybe the peddler just wants the king to know he's

alive. Maybe the king can give him some wisdom? Maybe the
king can help the peddler understand how to feel more satisfied, maybe — "

"Daddy, the peddler has to do this by himself, okay? I want
a monster story tomorrow. Let's go! I'll race you! If I win, I
get to choose the bagel for Mommy — *and* I get a cinnamon
raisin!"

EPILOGUE

Another long, icy winter. It's been nearly a year since I wrote in my Brady journal, but tonight I'm back here at the Pier 27 Lounge, watching the Super Bowl. And the Patriots and Tom Brady are in it this year! But right now things are not looking good. It's late in the third quarter, and we're down by ten points. And the defending champion Seattle Seahawks have the ball.

Before I got here, before the start of the game, I drove our Volvo station wagon to the supermarket and picked up a small cartful of canned goods, a couple of bags of rice, and then a serving tray of cut fruit, veggies, and dips. I brought them to WARM, our local shelter. I've been meaning to come here every Sunday, but I've only made it a couple of times so far.

The guy in the kitchen wore a Patriots hat and a Patriots jacket.

"How are you feeling about tonight?" I said.

"I don't know. I just don't know," he said. "Nervous, if you want to know the truth."

I went into the sitting room to see what the scene looked like in preparation for the game, but no one had settled in yet because it was still two hours before kickoff. On the coffee table, I picked up a worn copy of *Men's Health* magazine from last summer. On the cover was Russell Wilson, the young quarterback for Seattle. He was surrounded by the headlines: "Muscle by Russell: Build Big Arms Fast!" and "Scary Good Sex! Do You Dare?" and "Grit: Why It Matters, How You Can Get More, p. 150." These teasers were in bold caps in blue and green, the colors of the Seahawks.

Over the off-season, twenty-four-year-old Russell Wilson enjoyed a leap of fame similar to what Tom Brady experienced over a dozen years ago with his own first Super Bowl win. Very little was made of the fact that Wilson was only the second African American quarterback to win the big game. Or that he and his young wife were divorced not long after the victory. Meanwhile, Brady and Bündchen flipped their eco-chic mansion in Los Angeles, selling it for $40 million to the hip-hop artist and businessman Dr. Dre. For our part, Lisa and I sold our Volkswagen Vanagon to a dreamer and body shop mechanic in South Florida. He plans to fix it up and ship the old ride to Hawaii. He wants to live out of it for a while on a beach.

Also over the summer the sportswriters and analysts continued their talk about Brady's title window closing and how he is no longer an "elite" quarterback. Sparking further doubt, New England drafted a young quarterback named Jimmy Garoppolo in the second round. The rookie looked so promising that they traded away the previous backup, Ryan Mallett. In an interview just before the season began, Brady answered the usual question this way: "When I suck, I'll retire. But I don't plan on sucking for a long time."

This 2014 season began with an ugly loss in Miami. Once again, Brady had new, young unproven receivers, and a week before the opener, cold-blooded Bill Belichick traded Logan Mankins to the Tampa Bay Buccaneers. Mankins had been Brady's most-trusted offensive lineman. It seemed that once more Brady was beginning all over again for one final run with a new cast of characters. For that elusive fourth Super Bowl ring. The season continued poorly, and then the Patriots got embarrassed on Monday Night Football by the Kansas City Chiefs. They got beaten so badly that Brady was benched in the fourth quarter for the rookie—who threw a touchdown to Gronk. Several sportswriters penned Brady's epitaph. But then, just like last season, the Patriots went on a winning streak. They pummeled a string of the league's best teams, including the Denver Broncos. And unlike last year, the majority of the Patriots, including Gronk, stayed healthy. In the playoffs New England squeaked past the Baltimore Ravens— Brady led the team back twice from fourteen-point deficits —and then in the following game the Patriots obliterated the Colts again, just like last year, except this time Indianapolis had traveled the week before to Denver and knocked off the Broncos and a Peyton Manning figure that seemed a weakened shadow of himself.

Now here they are, in the Super Bowl, with a chance for that fourth trophy. Despite their relentless success, Brady and Belichick haven't been able to secure an NFL championship for over a decade. And over the last two weeks there have been leaked rumors alleging that the Patriots, maybe even Brady, illegally deflated the footballs against the Colts in order to grip the leather a little better in the rain. All three national news networks featured the scandal, dubbed "Deflategate." It has sparked a media obsession and an explosion of hatred against the Patriots. Brady has been accused of being a liar and a cheater. The *New Yorker* magazine ran a piece titled "The Humiliation of Tom Brady." I'm still holding out hope that somehow the quarterback didn't do anything too nefarious.

So after I dropped off the food this afternoon, I drove the Volvo to Pier 27. I was afraid I wouldn't be in time to get a good seat to watch the game, but it was less crowded than I expected. Loud Brady Lady and her husband weren't here, nor was Gangly John. The heavy hitters from Steelers Alley were on their way out, to watch the Super Bowl at home. I was able to say hello to Dr. No-No, sitting at his table, and to Mr. Little, who was slumped at his usual stool at the end of the bar. Dolphins Guy was on his stool, too. When I walked toward the seat I like by the vertical support and found it already claimed, Dolphins Guy greeted me kindly and joked: "That's what you get when you're not here every week."

Which is true. I haven't been coming in all that much this season. I've been mostly listening to the games on the radio while trying to get stuff done at home, such as overhauling our back fence or working on the little boat we bought to hopefully get Alice, Lisa, and me out onto the river more often. I took the fall off from teaching, too, so I tried to be more productive with other work.

I found a seat at a table close to Nick Name. I parked it right under where the autographed poster of the New England Patriots cheerleaders used to be, which they've replaced with a chalkboard listing the soup of the day.

"Vanagon now van-a-gone, eh?" Nick declared when he caught my eye.

"Good one," I said.

Brady is playing in his sixth Super Bowl tonight, the first quarterback in history to do so, but despite playing fairly well in the first half, he also threw an early, awful interception in the Seahawks end zone, and then he threw another one a couple of minutes ago, trying to force it to Gronk. The Seattle offense capitalized in only a few plays. The momentum has shifted hard in the wrong direction: 24–14 Seahawks.

Oh! Huge play! Patriots defensive end Rob Ninkovich just stormed up the middle and sacked Russell Wilson. We needed that! Seattle will need to punt. But there's less than twelve minutes to go in the game, still down by ten.

A stat just flashed on the screen explaining that no Super Bowl champion has ever come back from ten points in the fourth quarter.

The bar is eerily quiet. Everyone here is rooting for the Patriots—Dolphins Guy, Dr. No-No, even the bartender who normally wears a Jets jersey has a Gronk shirt on tonight.

People are concentrating. The vibe, to be frank, is somewhat depressing. It is a mixture of feeling like something bad is going to happen and like we are the misfits who weren't invited to the Super Bowl party. And we all know we are the ones who hate Super Bowl parties, because not enough people there are focused on watching the game.

"Stick a fork in us," Mr. Little says. "Seattle hasn't given up more than a touchdown in a fourth quarter in the last eight games. Know why they're the best D in the league? Because what they usually do in the second half is shut teams out. Goose eggs."

On the other side of the bar, at a table near the snack shelf, sit two men about my age. One has a gray goatee and wears a white Tom Brady jersey. The other has glasses and a faded red Pats sweatshirt from the Patriots' first Super Bowl in 2002. They're a little drunk and talking loudly over the commercials.

"The big question," the guy with the glasses says, "is if you'd trade lives with Tommy if it had to be forever? No going back."

"Leaving my kids?" says the friend wearing the number-twelve jersey.

"Yes, right now. You're the same person, your same mind—"

"Belichick would be disappointed, because I'd suck—"

"Well, yeah—but, no. You can still play football."

"At Brady's stage right now, like this night? Or in 2007?"

"Or maybe 2004 right after the third ring. You'd get the glory, but then you'd have to suffer all this decline talk and all this bullshit about how if they don't win tonight it's because of Spygate or Deflategate or whatever the haters have been piling on about. The two big disappointments to the Giants. Sitting on the bench and watching those catches on the Jumbotron. Maybe another loss tonight. But whatever. Your mind inside his. But you can still play football."

The man wearing the Brady jersey becomes thoughtful. And a little sad. As if his answer commits himself to the act. "Yep," he says. "I guess I would. But only if I get to start as him in 2001. Aw, shit. Who am I kidding? I'd do it right now. Even as he starts to wear out. I'd do it as he, or I, throws a pick-six right now to cocky young Richard Sherman. It's still better than anything I got."

The two friends drink ceremoniously. They turn back to the game as Brady and the offense take the field.

I'm thinking that I sure would like to play one game as Tom Brady. And I'd like to walk down the street just once as him, to take a blissful bath in that respect and adoration. And I still would really like to catch a few passes from Tom in some Sunday MFL game with the rest of the boys. But I'm also realizing, at last, that this would do it. I do not want to switch lives with Tom Brady.

The kind woman who once got me a napkin just walked past my table with a plate of pizza. She smiled at me and patted my shoulder in that way nice, friendly people do.

Mr. Brady, how about you and Wes Welker—and Lenny, Hoss, and I—we'll go for a little sailboat ride? To Hawaii. You buy the boat, okay? We'll do the rest. And Bono. Let's invite Bono. You know him? I have some questions that I'd really like to ask that man.

We at Pier 27 stare up at the television as Brady barks directions and some one zillion other people around the world also wait for him to call for the football. It's first down on the Patriots thirty-two.

"Here you go, Comeback Kid," says Nick Name.

"Ready the fork," whimpers Mr. Little.

"C'mon, Tommy!" shouts Loud Brady Lady, out of breath, hustling in with her husband. They're still bundled in their winter coats and Patriots ski caps.

The quarterback steps back to pass, can't find anyone open, holds on to the football too long, and gets hammered in the backfield for a huge loss. Ugh.

"TB12 like needs to retire yesterday," declares a woman in her twenties, looking up from her phone.

Brady flings a screen pass on second down, which goes for only a few yards. Not even back to the original line of scrimmage.

"No, no, no, no, no! What are they doing?! Took that one right out of the Redskins playbook," shouts our neighborhood dentist.

Chins are on tables.

"Dammit!" shrieks Loud Brady Lady, still standing.

This third and long feels like it's the game. It feels like if they have to punt here, it's over. Like Tom Brady's whole career will be defined on this one play: he's the greatest ever or he's the one who just couldn't win the big one as he got older.

Thomas Edward Patrick Brady Jr. points to a linebacker. He raises his left knee. He shouts directions and points again across the line at another defensive player. Split wide to his left, he's got Edelman, Amendola, and Gronk.

"C'mon, Tom-AY!" shouts the guy with the gray goatee and the number-twelve jersey. He stands up on his chair and turns to all of us. "One more miracle in this life. For us, right, Tom-AY!? Do not hang your heads. Right? We are going to win this game! One more ring, baby. Do not hang your heads. We are going to win this game."

ACKNOWLEDGMENTS

Thank you first and foremost to Lisa for her vast patience and support. She is the most significant person in my life: I love her and Alice "to Pluto and back."

Thank you to Stacey James of the Patriots, whose time and good humor made so much possible. For the gift of their time and expertise, I'm grateful to those who agreed to interviews and to be featured in the book. Several others who lent generous assistance to my pilgrimage but whose names do not appear within the book include Joe Reynolds, Donna Spigarolo, Sheri and Tim Grills, Mark Palmerino, and the merry filmmakers of *Catch It!* I'm grateful to all at the Pier 27 Lounge —in the hopes they'll forgive the poetic license—and to Jim Carlton, Mary K. Bercaw Edwards, and all at Williams-Mystic for institutional support and for making possible my research leave.

The book came to publication largely because of the savvy and experience of Laurie Abkemeier and the kind support and encouragement of Stephen Hull. I'm grateful to editing assistance and fact-checking from Sean Glennon, Rebecca Kessler, Seth King, Lisa Gilbert, and other family and friends who read and provided suggestions for the manuscript. Editors Peter Fong and Glenn Novak were once again an author's best friends.

To research this book, I turned to pro-football-reference .com, as well as the websites and publications created and maintained by the New England Patriots, ESPN, *Sports Illustrated*, and the NFL. I am indebted in particular to six football books for different aspects of their content, message, and style: Charles Pierce's *Moving the Chains: Tom Brady and the*

Pursuit of Everything, Frederick Exley's *A Fan's Notes*, George Plimpton's *Paper Lion*, Sean Glennon's *Tom Brady vs. the* NFL and *This Pats Year*, and Stephen J. Dubner's *Confessions of a Hero-Worshiper*.

And thanks to you, too, Tom.